Courageous:

Students Abolishing Abortion in this Lifetime

Kristan Hawkins

meant it. I said, "I promise you, that even if no one else cares about abortion, and if it takes me the rest of my life, I will end abortion for our daughter Jessica" (we knew that our child was a girl because the abortionist said to my girlfriend afterward, "By the way, your baby was a little girl"). And I know now that no one person can defeat the Culture of Death. But I really meant it at seventeen, that I would through my own will end abortion. And I believed it.

When I got back to my duty station—I was stationed at Schofield Barracks, Hawaii—I figured out how to get started. I said, "I'm gonna start knocking on doors" (I knew the Mormons and the Jehovah's Witnesses would knock on my mother's door, and she would talk to them). Just off Schofield Barracks there was all this housing, full of Filipino immigrant farm workers. I would knock on their doors and the workers would open the door, "Haole, what do you want?" I was this skinny kid with a shaved head and ugly PX civilian clothes, and I'd say: "I wanna talk to you about abortion. Can we talk about abortion? Do you know it's legal?" And they'd look at me like I was crazy, but sometimes they'd pour me Coors Light in a cup with ice, and we'd talk. Sometimes they'd slam the door in my face, but most of the time they agreed with me that abortion was a horrible crime that must be stopped

This was my plan! I would just knock on doors for the rest of my life on my off time. That's all I could think of. Then one day I got an angry call to my barracks. This woman was *mad*. She demanded, "Are you the man going around neighborhoods saying you represent us?" She gave the name of her organization. I said, "No, Miss, I've never heard of you. I've never said I represent you."

She said, "Well, yes, you are." I responded, "Miss, I've never heard of you guys. How would I say I represent you? I've never heard of you." She said, "You're Jason Jones, right? You gave your

As soon as he'd said that word, a sergeant reached over my shoulder and hung up the phone. So I punched him. Another drill sergeant grabbed me, but he saw that I was crying, just saying over and over again, "He killed my baby! He killed my baby!" They pulled me into my captain's office and threw me in a chair. At the sight of me falling apart like this, my captain—a big army ranger —looked pretty broken up himself.

I managed to form some sentences: "Sir, call the police, my girlfriend's father killed my child." And he asked me to explain what happened. And as I did he looked confused and he said, "Private. Why would I call the police? Don't you know that abortion is legal?" And you know, I didn't.

Although I was just an E1 private making three hundred dollars a month I did know one thing—that human life began at fertilization. That information was not above my pay grade. And I knew that my child was a human being. My captain must have been pro-life, maybe a Christian, because he soberly and sympathetically gave me a Sparks Notes version of *Roe v. Wade*. Then he handed me a roll of quarters for the phone and said, "I want you to go to the PX; I can't have you disturbing the whole battalion." I walked to the PX, hearing again the sound of my girlfriend sobbing, feeling our loss in my gut. The thought of that baby had kept me going, every grueling day of basic training. My heart was broken.

And my mind was reeling. What really knocked the wind out of me, what was really incomprehensible, was that what had happened to my baby was perfectly *legal*. That wouldn't sink into my head. It was too insane. I got to the payphone, and I called her back. We stayed on until every quarter ran out and the mechanical voice said, "You have sixty seconds. Please deposit more change." But I didn't know what to say, because she was still crying. And so I said the only thing I could think of that might comfort her. And I

So that's what we did. I went to the recruiter's office; I got the paperwork, which I needed my mother and my high school principal to sign. Now, out of five hundred and sixty-five students at Amos Alonzo Stagg High School, I was number five hundred and sixty-five. So my principal was quite happy to sign that piece of paper. My mother, with five kids, was also quick to sign the paper, with very few questions asked.

When I got to basic training, I didn't go to church. I tried to once, but it was just too much for me to bear. In fact, I realized I'd rather do anything else. So I asked the drill sergeants, "When the rest of you guys go to church, can I stay back and clean something?" They agreed, so I took on pots and pans duty, which nobody wanted. I discovered that the station was right next to a freezer where the drill sergeants would hide ice cream bars. I realized that if I took those ice cream bars, packed them in buckets of ice, and snuck them upstairs, when the soldiers came back from church I could trade them. "You shine my shoes for a week? Okay, here's an ice cream bar. You polish my brass for a week? Okay, here's an ice cream bar. You make my bed...." And so skipping church turned out to mean that I didn't have to polish my brass, shine my shoes, or make my bed. Not the best start for my moral education....

I was almost finished with basic and advanced infantry training and getting ready to graduate, and go home. I'll never forget the day—it was a Sunday when I was cleaning pots and pans while everybody else was busy praying. A friend came running in and said, "Jones, your girlfriend's on the phone and she's crying." So I ran out, knowing that I wasn't supposed to leave my station or answer the phone. But I picked it up, and she was crying, as I have never heard a woman cry before. Ever. The only way that I can explain it is that her *soul* was crying. And she kept saying over and over and over again, "I'm sorry, I'm sorry, I'm sorry. It wasn't me." And then her father said, "Jason," over the other line, "I know your secret, and your secret's *gone*. She had an abortion."

FORWARD

It was two days before my seventeenth birthday, a Saturday morning, the day after a football game in which I'd played. So I was tired and sore, but I could smell breakfast coming from downstairs and somebody was walking up the stairs. I was half asleep. The door opened: it was my girlfriend, I smiled, of course —but from the look on her face I could see that this wasn't called for. This was a serious moment. I steeled myself.

After a few long seconds, she looked up at me and said, "I'm pregnant." That woke me up quick. We sat there in my bedroom, two young teenagers. My room was still a boy's place, hung with football posters, sneakers, and baseball gloves strewn across the floor. But there I was, sitting next to my pregnant girlfriend. I knew all of a sudden I'd lost the right to keep on being just a boy.

My girlfriend went to an all-girls Catholic school and looked ahead to college, while I was dreaming of college football and a career in the NFL. We each had a plan for our lives. It was time to scrap those plans.

We strategized together figuring out how to take care of the new life we created. It felt completely natural and, incomprehensibly, even a little exciting: Our adult lives were starting much sooner than we had planned, but we'd figure it out. So here's what we decided: I could drop out of high school to join the army (a friend of mine had just done the same). My girlfriend would keep things secret, wear baggy sweaters and take vitamins until I got back from basic training and then we would be together—and I'd take care of all three of us.

"We know through painful experience that freedom is never voluntarily given by the oppressor; it must be demanded by the oppressed. Frankly, I have yet to engage in a direct-action campaign that was 'well timed' in the view of those who have not suffered unduly from the disease of segregation. For years now I have heard the word 'Wait!' It rings in the ear of every Negro with piercing familiarity. This 'Wait' has almost alwasy meant 'Never.' We must come to see, with one of our distinguished jurists, that 'justice too long delayed is justice denied."

- Martin Luther King, *Letter from Birmingham Jail*

ACKNOWLEDGMENTS

To Kristina, thank you for making this book a reality.

To the entire team at Students for Life of America, thank you for dedicating your lives to standing beside me, your crazy leader, as we fulfill our vision of abolishing abortion in our lifetime.

To Tina, I don't know where we would be without you.

To Ray, thank you for taking a chance on us.

To my family, thank you for the sacrifices you make.

To the students we work with, each of you are my heroes. You inspired this book. It is an honor to stand beside you in the greatest human rights campaign our world has ever known.

"Accustom yourself to look first to the dreadful consquences of failure; then fix your eye on the glorious prize which is before you; and when your strength begins to fail, and your spirits are well nigh exhausted, let the animating view rekindle your resolution, and call forth in renewed vigour the fainting energies of your soul."

- William Wilberforce

CONTENTS

"The real damage is done by those millions who want to 'survive.' The honest men who just want to be left in peace. Those who don't want their little lives disturbed by anything bigger than themsevles. Those with no sides and no causes. Those who won't take measure of their own strength, for fear of antagonizing their own weakness. Those who don't like to make waves - or enemies. Those for whom freedom, honour, truth, and principles are only literature. Those who live small, mate small, die small. It's the reductionist approach to life: if you keep it small, you'll keep it under control. If you don't make any noise, the bogeyman won't find you. But it's all an illusion, because they die too, those people who roll up their spirits into tiny little balls so as to be safe. Safe?! From what? Life is always on the edge of death; narrow streets lead to the same places as wide avenues, and a little candle burns itself out just like a flaming torch does. I choose my own way to burn."

- Sophie Scholl, Co-Founder of The White Rose and Holocaust Victim

Kortney and her preborn daughter Sophy were immediately killed, and Jon died in the hospital on October 18, 2011.

Our logo at SFLA is a candle lighting another candle, because that is our mission: to inspire, train, and equip this new generation of pro-life leaders who we believe will abolish abortion, those leaders like Jon. The best way to sum up Jon and Kortney's lives is to say that they lived their lives as such a candle, lighting candles, thousands of them, everywhere they went.

I have one picture of Kortney that I keep in my daily planner of her holding two twin little babies she once saved by simply taking a scared young woman out to breakfast and to a local pregnancy help center. Just a week before the accident, I received an email from a new Students for Life group that Jon helped start in Florida, telling me that he inspired them to have a vigil in front of a local abortion facility and that, on their first day, they had helped a scared, young woman change her mind and choose Life.

We know that even though Jon, Kortney, and Sophy are no longer here on this earth, they are still saving lives as the candles they lit are now lighting others. This book is dedicated to the memory of our courageous teammates, friends, and fellow abortion abolitionists: Kortney, Sophy, and Jon.

- Kristan Hawkins & the SFLA team

Not long after she started at SFLA, Kortney got engaged to Ben, and the entire SFLA team ended up not only helping paying for but happily cooking all of the food for her wedding. We loved her and still do. Kortney got pregnant on her honeymoon and found out she was having a baby girl, who she and Ben named Sophy.

Jon Scharfenberger was an amazing inspiration. I met Jon at a pro-life leader meeting one spring at Ave Maria University in Florida. He introduced himself as the president of the Students for Life group, and I immediately asked why he hadn't applied to intern with our team. After a little convincing, Jon applied and was accepted as a 2010 SFLA Missionary for Life, and he spent nine weeks in Washington, D.C. that summer with SFLA. Because Jon was assigned to work with me during his time in the SFLA office *(no easy task)*, I got to know him really well.

During a trip to Ave Maria the following spring, I told Jon that a job was waiting for him at Students for Life when he was ready. After graduation, he took an internship with National Right to Life in the summer and then started with us full-time in August. Jon was tasked with starting and leading our new initiative, *Pregnant on Campus*, which we designed to help pro-life student groups provide pregnant and parenting students on campus with all the information and help they need so abortion is never chosen because of a "lack of options." Jon had to take this vision out of my head and make it a reality. He was so trustworthy and put in long hours to make the project come alive. He was also the only man in the office and loved every minute of it.

On October 8, 2011, Jon, Kortney and two other pro-life activists were driving home from a Students for Life training conference in Macon, Georgia and were struck head-on by a drunk driver.

Our Dedication to Kortney and Jon

I met Kortney Blythe Gordon about six years ago when SFLA was just getting off the ground. I was speaking at a Students for Life training at a little Catholic college in California and in walked this group of hippies: decked out in long hair, flowery skirts, dreadlocks, the whole deal. I misjudged them and thought they were pro-abortion supporters, but they turned out to be the Survivors of the Abortion Holocaust team, a group of young people that educates college students on the horrors of abortion. Kortney was the leader of these "hippies," and we met then but never got to know each other until she moved across the country to work at another pro-life group in the Washington, D.C. area.

I had kept tabs on Kortney and heard great things about her work in the pro-life movement. One day, a friend who knew I was looking to hire a passionate pro-lifer for a position at SFLA called to say that Kortney was looking for a job. I asked her to interview and hired her immediately.

Kortney excelled as the Field Director for SFLA. Her job was hard, but she jumped right in and did a wonderful job. She knew exactly what needed to be done to train and inspire this generation of young people, and every student she worked with loved her. She was 100 percent dedicated to our mission and passionate about our cause, and it showed daily in the joy she brought to her work and our team. So often, pro-life students on campus think they are all alone in their fight against abortion but meeting Kortney was a huge "shot in the arm" to each of them. She was a true relationship builder.

number to so-and-so, right? And you're going door to door talking to people about abortion." I said, "Yes!" She said, "We're Hawaii Right to Life, that's what we do!" I stopped being defensive and was thrilled. "You mean there's a group? There are *more of us*?"

Before I got out of the army, one of my officers found out what I was doing. He'd heard rumors. He called me into his office, he said, "Private, I am hearing something very strange. I hear that in your off time sometimes you go around neighborhoods harassing civilians about abortion." I said, "Yes, sir, I do that." He said, "Are you crazy?" I said, "No, sir." So I told him what I wanted to do— to end abortion in America.

He stared at me and thought for a moment and said, "Well you know as an officer I was taught that if we had a big goal we needed a big plan. You start with your goal and you work your way back, step by step. You need a plan. Go write a plan. This is a big thing you're trying to do."

So I went and I wrote this hugely ambitious plan. I brought it back to him, and I said, "There's the plan, sir. This is how I'm gonna end abortion." He said, "This is a good plan. Work the plan. Work the plan for the rest of your life and maybe you'll achieve your goal." When I got out of the army, I started to work the plan. And I have been working the plan ever since. Of course, God throws me plenty of curve balls, and the plan has to change to suit the political changes in our country. But everything I do, in every sphere of my life and career, is guided by the central purpose that I found at age 17, because of my lost daughter Jessica - promoting the incomparable worth of the human person.

I went to University of Hawaii, started the pro-life student group and became chairman of the Young Republicans. It was as a college student—still an atheist, a fan of Ayn Rand actually—that I discovered just how much courage it can take to defend the value of human life. The purveyors of the culture of death on campus—the most vocal being the aging faculty and abortion industry hucksters, refuse to acknowledge that you're trying to defend the dignity and incomparable worth of the human person. The hippy reenactors will cast you as someone trying to ruin everyone's fun —to turn "harmless" hook-ups into life-changing catastrophes. Your mission is to get them to understand that "hook ups" in dirty dorm rooms are not worth denigrating the dignity of the human person or denying transcendent moral values such as justice, love and compassion.

Now that I'm making movies in Hollywood, people come up to me and congratulate me for my courage. Do you know what I tell them? "Compared to a college campus, being pro-life in Hollywood is easy. You know who is courageous? Those pro-life student activists. They are the ones on the front lines."

It is essential that pro-life young people stay bold and stay active. One thing to remember is that for every person who joins a student pro-life group or speaks up for our cause, there *are at least 100, maybe 1,000* more who silently agree with us. This is true even on the college campus—but especially true in the rest of society *(including your future bosses, co-workers, and potential spouses).* Social science bears this out. In 2012, the Gallup Poll found that only 41% of Americans identified themselves as "pro-choice," while 50% said they were "pro-life." Those are the best poll numbers that the pro-life position has had since Gallup started asking people this question in 1995, and the trend continues in our direction. The truth, that life is sacred, is graven in the human heart, and no lie can prevail against it forever.

I learned that lesson from reading one of the most powerful books I've ever come across, Pope John Paul II's autobiographical *Memory and Identity*. It was the last book he wrote before he died. In it, that Pope wrote about the three great ideologies of evil that he faced in his life: Nazism, Communism, and the Culture of Death. And he pointed out that in his own lifetime, there was a point when Nazi ideology seemed unbeatable. The Nazis had conquered most of Europe, were menacing Britain, were rolling straight for Moscow, and starting up their machinery for exterminating their enemies. People who lived under Nazi occupation had every reason to think its power would last indefinitely. But in fact, that regime was destroyed after only 12 years in power. So much for the Thousand-Year Reich.

Next, the Pope pointed out how Communists, who did much of the fighting against the Nazis and then filled their shoes as conquerors and tyrants, looked absolutely unconquerable. Communism rolled over Eastern Europe, then conquered China, and exported its agents and its armies to every corner of the globe, arming itself with nuclear weapons that could wipe out the human race.

Then in 1989, the Communist colossus collapsed from within. It had been built upon a bedrock of lies about the human person, so human beings eventually rejected it. We were born to know the truth, and something in our soul is repulsed by lies. This awakening takes work and it takes time. But it is ultimately unstoppable.

Now a whole generation has grown up free in countries like Pope John Paul's Poland—in time to face what the Pope called the third great evil of our century, the Culture of Death. It seems too deeply entrenched to be dislodged. Our culture's elites embrace it as a gospel that can't be questioned. Our government funds and promotes it, not just here but around the world—as the Soviets once pushed Communism. As I write this, the federal government, through the Obama administration's HHS mandate, is threatening with closure any institution—religious or not—that will not comply with the Culture of Death by funding abortion-causing drugs in their employee health insurance plans.

The mission at hand can look challenging. But as Pope John Paul would remind us, they looked even grimmer in 1940, and again in 1948. And those two empires of lies came tumbling down. So will this one—if we make it our life's work to share the dignity, beauty, and incomparable worth of the human person.

I understand now that I will never be able to keep that promise I made as a naive 17-year-old high school dropout to single handedly end abortion. But I do know that all of us working together will see in our lifetime a transformation of our culture in to a Culture of Life. That's why I love the work that Students for Life of America does. They do what is absolutely necessary for this transformation. They inspire and train this generation of abortion abolitionists - the generation who survived abortion themselves but are now targeted by the abortion industry to destroy the next generation. Students for Life of America knows that college campuses are the Ground Zero for this transformation, and they are the only organization doing this critical work. It is an honor to stand beside them.

I know that if all of us commit our lives and resources to this, the greatest human rights cause of our age, we will see full legal protection for the human person, from the child in the womb to the child in her mother's arms, from the embryo to the elderly, in our lifetime.

Jason Jones is a human rights activist, president of IAmWholelife.com, Co-Executive Producer of Bella, *Producer of* Crescendo, *and Associate Producer of* The Stoning of Soraya M.

INTRODUCTION

"Never underestimate what one person can do. One student can make a difference; can transform a campus, an entire city, an entire state, literally our entire nation." - David Bereit, 40 Days for Life

You know the people in this book - they are your classmates, your co-workers, friends, and even family members. They are the heroes that aren't praised on the front pages of newspapers or during the evening news, yet it is precisely their stories that need to be told.

Maybe you don't even know that your friend is a birth mother or that your co-worker is a survivor of abortion or that weird-looking older man who sits alone on the back pew is a sidewalk counselor.

These are the stories of ordinary individuals who have done extraordinary, courageous deeds, and I am thrilled that their stories are being told, many for the first time, in this book.

The original idea for this book was that we at Students for Life of America (SFLA) wanted a way to show the world and the pro-life movement the incredible work going on every day across the country by young people that you will most likely never hear about.

Most of what we do at SFLA won't make headlines on the news. It's the behind-the-scenes work of identifying pro-life student leaders, building relationships, teaching leadership skills, helping set up pro-life groups, and mentoring existing pro-life student groups that drives our team every day. It is through this mission that we come in contact with amazing individuals, some of whom you will meet in this book, who have sacrificed their time, careers, and lives to save babies they may never know and help women they just met.

This generation is the most pro-life generation since *Roe v. Wade* and *Doe v. Bolton* were handed down in 1973. We are more pro-life than our parents. Yet, the largest percentage of abortions are performed on college-age women, and it is these women that are the targets of the abortion industry and its Goliath, Planned Parenthood.

Our nation's schools are the Ground Zero of the abortion wars. Just ask Planned Parenthood, which has set their sights on students as young as the 1st grade to begin forming a relationship built on deceit and fear. And this is where the pro-life movement must be.

When SFLA first started, people thought it was "cool" that we did youth pro-life outreach but wanted to know what larger, national pro-life group we belonged to. We are and always have been a stand-alone national pro-life group because this is how important the youth of our nation are. They must be the priority, 100 percent of the time. By using the tools already at our disposal like technology *including ultrasounds, scientific studies, and social networking capabilities,* along with decades of pro-life education and our own personal experiences with abortion, we make it a priority to shape this generation that is already pro-life. We must shape this generation into the leaders they have been called to be that will ultimately be the ones to abolish abortion in our lifetime.

And make no mistake about it, this is the generation that will take the pro-life movement's dedication and sacrifice of the past 40 years and build upon it, to do whatever it takes to abolish abortion.

Students for Life's Vision

SFLA hosts a national sold-out conference every January for 2000 students around the anniversary of the *Roe v. Wade* and *Doe v. Bolton* decisions. In 2012, our theme was "Envision a World Without Abortion." It was the first conference of its kind in the pro-life movement to dedicate an entire event to the discussion of the question, "What will happen when abortion is abolished?" Can we once again live in a nation without abortion? Yes, it is possible.

At Students for Life of America, we believe that abolishing abortion in our lifetime is possible. However, it first starts with envisioning and believing in this possibility and working every day to make it a reality.

Anyone who has ever stood outside of an abortion facility knows that no woman ever wants to have an abortion. She runs to the abortionist when she feels that she truly has no other choice.

For the past 40 years, the pro-abortion movement has effectively pitted the mother against her baby. We want to transform our nation so that no mother will ever have to choose between her baby, education, finances, or relationship again. We're not saying it will be easy, but we can help this mother so she doesn't have to make that "choice."

To do this, we believe the pro-life movement must engage young people to lead with their creativity and passion for the cause, connect with those most vulnerable to the abortion industry's lies, and stop the abortions where they are happening - in our nation's schools.

This is a different kind of movement. We run Students for Life like a political campaign. Our office is vibrant and a little crazy at times. While we are loud and love rock music, we are 100 percent serious about our mission and work as a team utilizing dozens of white boards, maps, and Excel spreadsheets to strategize and track our progress. Despite the sometimes 15-hour days and weeks traveling on the road, we exhibit great joy in what we do because we know we can and we are making a huge impact. We have the best "jobs" in the world; we work full-time to save lives, change our culture, and transform this nation.

Why We Wrote This Book

Our first goal is that when you read through the book you will understand that momentum is on our side. And while the young people featured in this book are diverse – culturally, religiously, politically – they are serious abortion abolitionists. They have caught the vision.

Our second goal is that we hope this book serves as inspiration for you. When you read this book, you will see that these young people have ordinary, messy lives, yet have done extraordinary things. And you are in the pro-life movement, just like them, not for the glory but because you've been uniquely called to this cause. No matter who you are or how old or young you may be, you can make a real difference.

In this book, you'll read about Steve, an ordinary guy who just went to a rock concert that changed his world view and ended up facing a recall election as student body president because he refused to back down from his pro-life beliefs. You will read about

Melissa, a woman who survived unimaginable abuse at home and ended up living with nuns to escape her father, who forcibly aborted her siblings and had wanted her to succumb to the same fate. You will read about Julia, a girl who knows no fear and reaches out to women every day at abortion facilities, always offering help and the option to choose life. You will read about Amanda and Andrea, courageous birth mothers who placed their babies with adoptive parents. And you will read about Rebekah, a young girl who was raped and courageously chose life for her son.

We also hope this book inspires and serves as a thank you to the pro-life movement's leaders who have worked for the past 40 years to abolish abortion. Special thanks goes especially to Nellie Grey, who passed away while we were writing this book. Nellie started the annual March for Life in Washington, D.C. to commemorate the *Roe v. Wade* and *Doe v. Bolton* decisions and made attending the March the highlight of the year for many young people today.

And, thank you to all of my heroes who prepared and inspired me to lead this truly life-saving organization: Mom, Dad and Sharon, and to my husband, Jonathan, and sons, Gunner and Bear, who sacrifice their time with "Mommy" to allow me to continue this calling.

For Life,
Kristan Hawkins

THE EXCEPTION: REBEKAH BERG

"Courage is not the absence of fear but rather the judgement that something else is more important than fear." - Ambrose Redmoon

I was finally living on my own, away from my family for the first time and a freshman in college. I was a mere three months into my college career when my supposed "friend", a guy on the football team, asked me to watch a movie and then proceeded to rape me. But it wasn't until two years later that I was able to acknowledge it was rape and, by that time, I had born the son of my rapist.

I Was Raped

At college, I had a job as the assistant student athletic trainer, and because of that position, I got to know some of our school's football players. One of the football players that I had become friends with invited me to hang out with some of the other players and cheerleaders to "catch up." The plan was to go to see a movie with everyone. My friend who had invited me offered to pick me up and drive because I didn't have a car on campus.

Once he picked me up, we drove for what seemed like just a few minutes before he pulled into a dark park near our school. I assumed we were just meeting the others there until he turned off the engine and pushed a few buttons in his car making a video screen pop up from the dashboard. The movie was in his car, not at a theater with other friends. Since we were friends, I didn't think much of it being just him and I, but something in my gut told me this wasn't right. I was excited a guy wanted to spend time with me, but honestly I really didn't see it as more than friends. I did not like him more than a friend.

No less than ten minutes into the movie he starting kissing me and soon was on top of me. He was quickly finishing what he started even though I had asked him to stop several times. He looked up at me and said "let me finish or I will go get someone else." Helpless, I told him to continue because I couldn't bear the thought of him doing this to someone else. It wasn't that I felt a romantic connection to him or didn't want to be thrown aside, but rather I didn't want another girl to be put in this same situation. He was nearly finished and all I could think about was getting it over with as soon as possible.

Afterwards, he took me back to my dorm and I rushed up to my room and took the hottest shower that I could possibly bear. I remember just standing in the hot shower trying to erase what had just happened. I must have stood there at least 20 minutes. I felt dirty and no amount of water could get the feelings of his touch off of me.

I Didn't Fight Back

Throughout the fall semester, this "friend" of mine would call me to tell me he was on his way to pick me up. He would give me specific instructions on what to be wearing and when to meet him. I'm sorry to say that I met him every time. Every. Single. Time. It was the same routine with him. He would take me away from campus, have sex with me, and drop me back at my dorm.

After every instance, I went home thinking it was the last time and that I would refuse to meet him the next time he called. But then I thought that he would just call someone else and do the same things to them.

Reflecting on this time in my life, I have considered why I kept going back to him time and again, and I just don't have an exact answer. I do think I was mostly worried if I didn't meet him he would start doing this with someone else on campus. On the other hand, as awful as it sounds and even though I never liked him as more than a friend, I think I was glad to have the attention of a male. I liked it and hated it all at the same time. I was just an object to fill his needs and then to be discarded. We would casually talk during the car ride to and from campus, but there was never any deep conversation. Just the basic how are you, how are classes, how are you liking living here. If we saw each other on campus or at my job, it was a simple hello – no different than any other relationship I had with guys on campus. I remember always feeling dirty as I got ready and used when I came home.

Christmas break could not have come soon enough, and I was able to go home and get away from him, yet it wasn't until I came back for the spring semester that I realized I had missed a period. I confronted my friend when he returned from Christmas break and told him I thought I was pregnant. He took me to get a test and waited outside of the Wendy's as I anxiously peed on a stick. I was indeed pregnant.

Despite growing up learning about the development of a tiny preborn baby and helping my mom stuff envelopes for our state pro-life office, all of my ideas of being pro-life when it came to this baby went out the window. I was terrified. I thought if I told my parents that a) I was pregnant and b) the father was a black man, then my family would surely disown me.

The Abuse Continues

While we both agreed to end the life of our baby, the father went about it his own way. The first attempt at an abortion was when he took me to the original park where he had first raped me. He asked me to get out of the car and come around to his side and then he punched me as hard as he could in the stomach. I doubled over and screamed. There were other people at the park, and he warned me if I screamed again he would make sure it was my last. He punched me several more times before he took me back to my dorm.

Amazingly, I did not lose my baby.

The next week during one of my work shifts in the athletic trainer's office, he came in seeking treatment for a football injury. The trainer had to leave the room for a moment and left me alone with him. As I hooked him to the machine, he grabbed my arm, twisted it, pulled me to the table, and whispered his true intentions on the visit. He was going home to get money for an abortion and when he came back I better have the abortion set up. I knew by his tone and the look in his eyes that this wasn't an option for me. He got up and left as soon as he had made his demands.

Getting Help

I was so desperate for help at this point. I knew what an abortion was, but I couldn't bear telling my family the truth. I knew I had to tell someone what I was going through, so I didn't feel so alone. When I got back to my dorm, the girl across the hall was home. While I wasn't more than acquaintances with this girl, we did hang out on a few occasions with my roommate and her roommate, and she was very quiet and I knew she could keep a secret. She was alone and I just remember saying to her that "I need to talk to someone." I told her I was pregnant and was going to have an abortion.

She looked at me with kind eyes and sweetly said, "Tell me everything you know about abortion." I shared everything I knew. I explained what partial birth abortion was and how the gruesome procedure would be conducted. I am almost positive that I explained how big my baby was and what he or she was already capable of doing. At the end, I just looked at her teary-eyed and said, "I can't do this." She cried with me as I figured out what to do next.

This girl was an angel to me. She graciously called her own mom who helped find a home in a near-by city that I could live in until I gave birth. I didn't end up going to this home, but I did talk to a woman at the facility and discussed when I would want to come and how the program would work. There are options for women in my situation that I never knew about, and this girl was so helpful. I was truly in a difficult mental state where I was battling all kinds of emotions at once and to have someone with me who was level-headed and clear-thinking was truly a blessing.

With this girl sitting beside me, I had to face my family. I had already talked to this girl's mom as well as the pregnancy hotline and now I needed to tell my family. She made me call my mom and sat with me as I shared the news and ended up staying afterwards as well. It was difficult to say the least.

As I feared, my mom didn't want anything to do with me. I was her only daughter, at a Christian school and now pregnant by a black man. My parents were not racist and my brothers and I all had black friends growing up, but my parents still believed that inter-racial relationships were not acceptable.

The next 24 hours are still a blur. At some point, my mom called me back and told me to pack my things because my dad would be making the 14-hour drive to come and pick me up.

I left school before the baby's father came back to campus with the abortion money. I dropped a note in the mailbox for him with no information on how to reach me. After several weeks of harassing calls to my roommate, calls that had her in tears and afraid, I agreed to let him have my phone number. I didn't know what else I could do.

Once I had come home, I enrolled in the spring semester at a local university and started counseling at a local maternity house as well as started working at the state pro-life office. I was set on giving my baby life but placing my baby for adoption. Throughout this time, the father of my child, along with his own mother, would continue to call my home, harassing our family. Apparently he told his mom that we were in love and had been dating for some time. I definitely was not in love nor had we been dating, but it was his word against mine.

When I was six months pregnant, my mom forced me to go to our church's youth retreat. My dad and I were not speaking at the time and my mom just told me that she had already paid the money so I was going. Since I was living with my parents and couldn't escape their authority I had to go. I was running as far away as I could from God wondering why he could do this to me, why he allowed this to happen to me. I didn't want to face God, and I certainly didn't want to face my peers and other friends who didn't even know I was pregnant.

Even though I hadn't made it public that I was pregnant, at the retreat, a very close friend of mine, who happened to be a pastor, sat down beside me in the entryway into the meal hall and started talking about my preborn baby. I was a little shocked that he knew but figured my mom must have told him. He looked straight into my eyes and said, "you're keeping this child aren't you?" I broke down in tears. It was at that moment that I had the affirmation I was already this child's mother.

At that moment, I knew I was the mother of my child, but I wouldn't say that I felt like a mom. When I went to the maternity house for counseling, I would get so mad when I would tell the counselor that I was placing my baby for adoption. I knew what it meant – that I might not see my child again – or that if I chose an open adoption that I would see my child every so often, but my child would never know me as mom.

I had all of those thoughts that you typically hear as to why you should not keep a child conceived in rape – he will grow up and do this to other women as well, you will see the man's face every time you look at your child, you will never be able to love him. I didn't want to face those questions and choose to place my baby with an adoptive family in case they were true. I didn't know anyone that had been in my situation to confirm or deny my questions, so I assumed I was right since I had heard the same questions arise in others' minds.

The counselor tried to help me see every angle of my decision. Even though she was just doing her job, it was hard for me. If I said I was going to place the baby with an adoptive family, she would tell me I should mother. When I decided I was going to keep the baby and be a mother, she told me every reason why I would fail. I know now that she was just ensuring that I had thought of every possible scenario and was well prepared with either choice I made.

Before this youth retreat I had wondered, and I think that I had been wondering since I had started the counseling (when I was around three months pregnant) on whether or not I should mother. By the time I was six months pregnant and at this retreat, I was really considering it but didn't think my family would be supportive. I had resigned myself to the fact that adoption was my only choice without support. Yet when I was speaking with my friend/pastor, I decided at that point that I was going to raise my baby myself. When I did tell my mom, she was supportive unlike what I thought she would be, which was a pleasant surprise.

Acknowledging the Truth

Throughout the rest of my pregnancy, I continued to receive harassing phone calls from my baby's father and his family. Once my son had been born, the calls turned to letters with threats of taking my son away from me to threats of killing me. At the pro-life office where I worked, an attorney who was on our board came to know of my situation. She offered to take my case to protect me, pro bono. The only stipulation was I had to tell her every detail about what had happened, every gruesome detail she said.

As I shared what had happened, the humiliation and the fear, she stopped me and said, "Oh honey, you were raped." I corrected her and told her that the man that did this was a friend, so I wasn't raped. A friend would never do something like that. She knew I didn't believe her, so she had me report the incident to a detective in the city it happened in.

As I talked with the detective, the same words came out of her mouth. I argued with her as well, making the same claims that he was a friend. She then asked me a question that changed everything for me, "Did he ever tell you it was your fault that the sex had happened?" The simple answer was yes. The day after that night in the dark park, when we were supposed to be watching a movie with friends but when he forced himself on me, he said that very line. In fact, he told me that he had been high and it never would have happened if he hadn't been.

Besides, I leaned in towards him, so that meant I wanted him to have me, right? I was asking for it, wasn't I? If I didn't want sex I would have never agreed to hang out and watch a movie, right?

I learned that day that over 70 percent of rapes are done by a friend, someone that you already know. The assailant tells you it's your fault, and most victims of rape by a friend happen more than the one time. This was me. This was my story. It was no longer my fault, and I finally was able to process my thoughts and feelings once I came to terms with what had truly happened that November night.

My Son is the Exception

In the end, I decided to raise my son myself. As a single mother and with the help of those around me, I went to school, worked two jobs, and graduated college. I met an amazing man that has since become the most amazing father and dad to my son. We married our senior year of college and made the family I always wanted for my son and I. We have three children including my son.

My son is the product of rape, and he is the exception to the rule, as they say. Multitudes of women in my situation have had abortions, giving different reasons for their choice. But that child is still a child, no matter how he or she was conceived. I certainly did not choose to be raped and definitely did not choose to become pregnant. No more did my child ask to be conceived. I had no right to take his life because of the horrible situation that had happened to me.

The thought that he would bear the same genes of my rapist was one of the questions that continued to linger at my soul during my pregnancy. Was I going to birth another rapist? Was I doing more harm than good with giving him life? My own son's gentle spirit and thoughtfulness of others confirms that there is not a "rapist gene." When I look into my son's eyes, I only have love and have only loved him since he was laid on my chest after birthing him.

In the 10 years that I have been allowed to be his mom, he has given me only one look where I saw a resemblance to his biological father. It was gone as quickly as it came, and it never changed my feelings for him. If anything, it reminded me of how special of a child I have. I'm also so grateful for my pro-life friend who helped me choose life for my son. What if I didn't have that friend to talk to? Would my son be here today? I would miss his.....everything!

My son is now 10 years old. He's a great kid that loves sports. He plays football and basketball. He is a healthy, well-rounded, smart, funny, and happy child. I could not imagine my life without him in it. What may have looked like ashes has truly been turned to beauty. My son has made my life better. Isaiah 55:13b says it best: "You are an everlasting sign of what God can do."

Rebekah Berg is a work-at-home mom to three children, 9, 4, & 2 ½. She teaches skin care and cosmetics with the number one company in the world. She is married to the greatest man, Eric, who works hard to provide for his family. Rebekah loves to share her journey of becoming a mother whenever she can in hopes that abortion in cases of rape is no longer an exception to the rule. She believes that others need to hear her story because it is then that they can truly know the facts and make an educated decision and begin to help others.

THE CONFIDANT: GINA FAZENBAKER

"Words can never adequately convey the incredible impact of our attitudes toward life. The longer I live the more convinced I become that life is 10 percent what happens to us and 90 percent how we respond to it." - Charles Swindoll

Nearly always, the most beautiful and courageous choices that people make are left off the front pages of newspapers, never talked about on television or posted on social media websites. In a small town in Pennsylvania I got to witness one of these choices and I am forever grateful for the opportunity for the small part I played in bringing a new life into this world.

It started when I was a freshman at Clarion University, located in a small town in Western Pennsylvania between Erie and Pittsburgh. To make friends, I would ask random students to have lunch with me. I saw Levi*, an international student, leaving the library one day and asked him to lunch. Even though we were, literally, from different sides of the world we had a lot in common. It was fun to talk to him and we became fast friends. Our professor even stuck us in groups together in class because he didn't want the student from across the globe to feel left out.

Because Levi was so far away from his family, he never had anywhere to go during the holidays. Because hanging out on a deserted campus during Thanksgiving and Christmas is no way to spend a break, I invited him back to my home for the holidays, and Levi soon became close to my family. When we both studied abroad and he returned back to the States before I did, he even stayed with my family when I wasn't there, and, when Levi got married, he and his wife lived with my family for awhile. My parents even added him to our family's cell phone plan, and he was in our Christmas card picture every year. He danced the mother-son dance with my mom at his wedding while my dad gave all the obligatory father of the groom speeches. For all intensive purposes, my parents treated him like one of their own children.

Levi was really more than my friend; he became a brother to me. But Levi was always getting into these pickles mostly because he didn't have much money.

I had graduated by the time Levi needed to find an apartment for his senior year and because of financial problems, he waited until the very last minute to go house hunting. Against my advice, he ended up moving into an apartment with two girls from the international program.

Soon after the fall semester started, one of Levi's roommates, Jen*, found out that she was unexpectedly pregnant; the father was a guy she had casually seen over the summer. Jen came from a country where her culture looked down on women who conceived a child out of wedlock. Jen knew that if family found out about her pregnancy, she would suffer severe consequences. Her parents would easily cut her off financially, she would not be able to finish school, and she would be forced to return to her country with very little hope for her or her baby.

Spreading the Pro-Life Message

My parents were involved in the pro-life movement when I was really little, so I was raised to be pro-life. From a very young age, I was ready to confront the other side about the horrors of abortion. When I was in kindergarten, I remember having a debate with my teacher as to why Bill Clinton's picture was on our wall. I knew how much he supported abortion and could not understand why we needed a photo of him in our classroom when he would not protect the littlest among us.

When I got to college at Clarion, there was a pro-life group there, but it was a really small one. Sometimes there were meetings when there were just a few students in attendance. Thankfully it was driven by a pro-life professor at the school, so we had strong support. I became the president of the pro-life group my sophomore year. I even got a pro-life love story out of my experience in the Students for Life group, since the vice president of the club would be the man I would later marry.

During my time as president, we had pro-life speakers come to campus, information tables set up often, and social events organized for group members. We could easily call up 50 people to volunteer for any given event. We even started a Pregnant and Parenting Program , which was developed to help students get the resources they need so that they didn't have to choose between staying in school or keeping their baby. By the time I graduated, our group was really active.

Since Levi and I were so close, he knew about abortion and had become strongly pro-life through our friendship and my involvement in the pro-life movement. The international students at Clarion were a very tight-knit group and looked out for each other. Levi was well respected and a leader in the international community and the other students really looked to him to see what he'd do with his roommate's unexpected pregnancy.

After she found out that she was pregnant, Jen sought advice from Levi, and he called me. He wanted to know how to talk to Jen and help her to see that choosing life for her baby would be the best option. Having been involved in the Pregnant and Parenting Program, I knew where to turn. I immediately told him to take her to the local pregnancy resource center where she could obtain tangible support, both relationally and practically, and receive counseling. That was a no brainer.

Jen was leaning towards abortion because she was living in a foreign country and financially dependent upon her parents. It was an extremely scary thing to face for her. She couldn't tell her parents she had been dating someone as she was supposed to have an arranged marriage, let alone that she had slept with this boyfriend over the summer and had become pregnant.

Initially, the other international students thought that Jen should abort the baby. They all knew her situation and how difficult it would be for her if her parents found out. However, Levi was supportive of both Jen and her baby. He cared for them and helped Jen see that abortion was not the way out of her situation.

Once Levi shared his conviction for life and the other international students saw that he was her rock, they too began to come around to side with Levi that Jen should indeed keep her baby.

Rallying around Jen and her baby

It was a difficult school year. Levi ended up getting mono and was sick for most of the semester. Jen got gestational diabetes. But no matter what, the students rallied around Jen and helped her throughout her pregnancy.

They cared for her like a family when she developed gestational diabetes and was sick. I was so moved to see how Levi and the other international students supported Jen and cared for her. They lent her money, transported her to doctor appointments, and picked up prescriptions.

Some students even pooled their money together to get the medicines Jen needed. They even threw her a beautiful baby shower that my family and I attended. I still have pictures of all of us at the baby shower, a pretty diverse bunch. And the students even incorporated some cultural traditions into the shower where my parents stood in for Jen's parents. It was such a wonderful show of support for Jen and her baby.

During Jen's pregnancy, Levi would often call me to ask for advice, and I was happy to help. But it was much to my surprise when towards the end of Jen's pregnancy, she asked me to be one of her birthing coaches. I had no idea what to do but was honored beyond belief!

Jen's due date was during finals week, and I took off a week of work to clean her apartment and make last minute preparations for the baby's birth and homecoming. I even went to buy Jen nursing bras – she had no idea what size to buy because all her bras were from her native country. I got all the last minute tasks done and, surprisingly, even learned how to fit a car seat into a car.

Thankfully, Jen also asked the nurse who was caring for her throughout the pregnancy to help during the birth. The birth of Jen's baby was one of the most amazing experiences of my life. I held her hand, the hand of a woman I barely knew, through an entire evening and night, and didn't let go until they moved her into the operating room for an emergency C-section.

And I was there when the nurses brought the little boy into the nursery. I can't describe what it was like, to hold the perfectly-formed, long, skinny fingers of this tiny little person who almost wasn't. What a wonderful feeling it was to know that I was able to play a small part of bringing this baby into the world.

Jen and the baby's father have since married and moved on. I can't say where they are now, but knowing that there is a precious two-year old boy with big brown eyes, a crop of black hair, and soft, mocha skin toddling around somewhere that I had a (small) part in protecting is one of the proudest and most surreal accomplishments of my life.

Gina Fazenbaker graduated from Clarion University in 2009 and was one of the original Students for Life of America missionaries. She is currently a youth worker at an after-school program.

*Names have been changed to protect identities.

THE SISTER: CAROLINE PILGRIM

"The only thing we're certainly not prepared to do is give in. ...Not violate our consciences, and not obey what we consider to be something immoral. That we're committed on." - Cardinal Timothy Dolan

I was three-years old when I felt Emma, age eight-months-after conception, squirming in my mom's uterus. I was the baby of family, the youngest of three girls, and I was looking forward to welcoming the newest member of the family. A few hours after Emma was born, mom and dad brought her home and put her on their bed and dad said, "Girls, come meet your sister." Emma was wearing a tiny pink beanie hat, already a stylish little girl; and I was in love. Growing up, Emma and I were best friends, and I have had the distinct advantage of knowing her since before she was born.

From a young age we humans know right from wrong. We know that death is death and that to kill someone is wrong. My family subscribed to the weekly Christian news magazine *World* which was not shy about informing its readership about key social issues. In multiple issues I saw growing up, *World* showed pictures of aborted babies. It was these graphic images, horrifying to a child, that let me see abortion and realize its gravity. Seeing images changes us and these photographs and articles about abortion changed how I saw my country and viewed right and wrong. I attribute seeing those images of abortion from such a young age to the passion that was ignited in me to save preborns from this unnecessary fate.

I was an Army brat, meaning my family moved around a lot. When we lived in the Washington, D.C. area, we went to the March for Life each January. The March commemorates the January 23, 1973

Supreme Court landmark *Roe v. Wade* and *Doe v. Bolton* decisions that legalized abortion in all nine months of pregnancy, for whatever reason.

Annually, up to half a million Americans attend the March for Life. Many women bravely attend and not only hold confessional signs that admit to aborting their children but also verbalize their regret in public testimonies. Each time I attended this gathering, it reinforced my belief that abortion was wrong and that life began much earlier than human eyes can see. When did my little sister, Emma, become Emma? It was before she was born and, in that moment, when only God was merging two cells together to create a unique person. I knew I had to protect the littlest people.

Finding my Calling

In 2008, just when the hype of then-Senator Barack Obama's presidential campaign was taking off, I enrolled in Wheaton College, which is just a little east of Chicago. Wheaton is a liberal arts Christian college where I was challenged spiritually and intellectually. The school is allegedly the "Harvard of Christian Colleges" and boasts that it has a history of transforming culture for Christ. This was precisely why I was more than a little concerned when the student paper published a poll indicating half of Wheaton's faculty would vote for then-Senator Obama for President of the United States.

For the informed voter in 2008, it did not require extensive research to quickly realize Senator Obama was unwaveringly pro-abortion, admitting that if his daughters became pregnant he wouldn't want them "punished with a baby." I assumed that my faculty also knew Obama had voted multiple times against the

"Born Alive Infant Protection Act," which was supposed to protect babies born alive after a botched abortion and allow them to receive medical care.

From the moment that the candidates were selected for the Presidential race, it seemed clear to me that the life issues trump all else. And if the leader of our nation, or any leader for that matter, does not value life at all its stages, they should not get our vote. And so, it was during the 2008 presidential campaign that I came to the conclusion that my life would be one devoted to protecting the preborn and stopping abortion. If my professors and my peers could not make the obvious connection between policies and politics that literally put to death the most vulnerable in our society, then I would be the one to tell them. It clicked for me then. I had found my calling.

Heading to Florida

For mainly financial reasons, I ended up leaving Wheaton College and transferring to the University of Florida in Gainesville in 2009. Gainesville is known mostly for its out-of-control, yet very fun, football culture. Before starting classes I drove to town to look for housing and noticed a Planned Parenthood 10 blocks from campus. I really wasn't as excited about the football culture as I was about actually being able to do something to protect preborns so close to where I lived.

You see, most Americans, especially college-aged and teens are unaware of Planned Parenthood's large profit margins from abortions, which can cost upwards of $500 each. And with the partying lifestyle of a college environment, it's not hard to imagine that many unplanned pregnancies happen. Planned Parenthood wants to be there to make a profit off of vulnerable women who see no other way out than to abort their child. So it didn't surprise me when I found out how close to campus Planned Parenthood had set up.

In fact, early in 2012, Students for Life of America actually did a study to see if Planned Parenthood targets the locations of their clinics in college areas. Data from previous studies had already shown that Planned Parenthood has over 60 percent of their clinics located in minority neighborhoods, so targeting colleges was not a far leap. The study found that indeed Planned Parenthood sets up over 75 percent of their clinics within a five-mile range of college campuses.[1]

At the University of Florida, I became an active member of the Pro-Life Alliance, an organization affiliated with the national Students for Life of America group. If I wasn't praying or sidewalk counseling outside of the Planned Parenthood abortion facility or studying, I was reading pro-life news articles and educating myself on abortion. On campus, I was able to raise awareness by tabling, coordinating speakers, or hosting fundraisers for the two local pregnancy resource centers.

On Wednesdays and Fridays, the Planned Parenthood would do abortions, so I made it a point to bring people with me to pray outside or sidewalk counsel. There were about 20 active members of our Pro-Life Alliance group including a small band of Catholic students that would go every Friday and pray a few rosaries. Often though, there would only be a handful of us.

---

[1] http://studentsforlife.org/files/2012/05/Abortion-Facilities-Target-College-Students.pdf

Abortion is a highly charged topic, and I did have confrontations occasionally on campus when doing pro-life work. One afternoon, I was setting up a table at the Reitz Collonade, the most heavily trafficked area on campus, giving out pro-life literature and talking to students about the Pro-Life Alliance's positions. Earlier that week, Live Action had released undercover videos of Planned Parenthood assisting sex traffickers, so I made a fact sheet about the investigation and was handing it out. That same day, the VOX (Voices of Planned Parenthood) group was also tabling about "sexual awareness" and the services of Planned Parenthood. I approached Tom, who was an officer in VOX and frequent "deathscort" volunteer at the local Planned Parenthood, and asked him about Planned Parenthood's services and how they reconciled providing women with health care while killing their preborn children.

I explained to Tom my passion for maternal fetal healthcare and how personal this issue is to me. I lost my own uncle and grandmother because of poor women's health. My grandmother died in childbirth in the 1960s. Tom candidly said, "Your grandmother would not have died if she had gone to a Planned Parenthood." This wasn't the last time I would hear hubristic, false statements from Planned Parenthood supporters. The reality is that Planned Parenthood doesn't do anything in terms of prenatal care or birthing live babies, and I could not imagine them saving my grandmother and her preborn child, my uncle.

Our culture considers college the time to find your identity, what you're good at, and what you should do with your life. You're supposed to "evolve ideologically" in college and explore new ideas. In college, I did find my identity and the purpose for my life. I found that people matter most, and it's passion to make sure each person has the right to live.

Going into Medicine

Since the time I was in high school, I knew I wanted to go into medicine. In 2004, my sister, Emma, crashed my family's 12-passenger van, and she was thrown out the window. She should have suffered serious traumatic injuries but thankfully only sustained cuts and bruises. It was intense, but I remained calm in the midst of the trauma. I liked knowing that I had the ability to stay calm during the traumatic event, and I knew medicine was something that felt like the right fit for me.

I am currently on the medical route and am enrolled in my second year of Physician Assistant School at Jefferson College of Health Sciences in Roanoke, Virginia. I will graduate in December 2013, and I plan on specializing in women's health.

Medical school is a new sort of challenge for my pro-life beliefs. It's not as black-and-white as it used to be. In college I had a job as tech at the health center, and I was given the opportunity to talk to a patient who was considering abortion. It was easy because I simply got to address her emotionally. I took her blood pressure and got to sit down and talk about why she wanted to end the life of her baby. But being a healthcare provider isn't always that easy. Patients have rights and autonomy, and there's more at stake in your career when you have firm convictions because I see how most do not share my beliefs.

My medical classmates truly do not believe that life is precious. In many conversations and in my classes, we obviously talk about end of life care and advance directives and medical and surgical abortions. In class, I see more time given to discussions about the elderly, specifically their medical needs. The general consensus among my classmates is that they are old and useless, vegetables almost, so it is "ok" to let them go. These are our grandmas and grandpas, our parents, and our friends. They have families of their own and each one have an undeniable dignity that is being willfully overlooked because their medical treatments are expensive and lengthy. Unfortunately that is the reality in my medical school and I imagine in most others as well.

Even though it's talked about less, abortion is still brought up. The prevailing attitude is that birth control is the answer to most problems. Have an irregular period? Go on birth control. Suffer from mind-bending PMS? Go on birth control. Have a sinus infection? Birth control is the answer. Okay, maybe not sinus pain, but the point is that birth control is held up in an unrealistic and idealistic light. I have personally observed attitudes from my fellow classmates that perpetuate ideas that all lower-income women need birth control, so they won't make more poor kids or that parents need to take a test to prove they are intelligent enough and well-equipped to handle a child before they can become pregnant. Thankfully, though, many students and professors don't think abortion is the answer, but they certainly believe it's a woman's choice and her body.

In this hostile environment, I came close to being expelled from PA school last year because I attempted to bring a pro-life OB/GYN to give a talk about "the struggle keeping abortion safe, legal and rare."

In December of 2011, I was contacted by Kristan Hawkins, the President of Students for Life of America, which is also the umbrella group for Medical Students for Life, to help facilitate an appearance on campus from Doctor John Bruchalski, or "Dr. B" as most people call him. Dr. B is a pro-life physician who has an obstetrics and gynecology practice in Northern Virginia, right outside of Washington, DC. His practice follows the teachings of the Catholic Church and does not prescribe birth control pills but helps women in crisis pregnancies, providing health care regardless of a woman's ability to pay. Dr. B used to perform abortions and now speaks at medical schools about how the pro-lifers and pro-aborts can work together to help make abortion a rarity. His talks are engaging and compassionate to both sides, and I really wanted to help get him to my campus so my peers could benefit from his knowledge and honest discussion.

I was friends with the Student Activities Coordinator on campus and another girl who works in the same office, and I talked to them in February about having Dr. B come and speak at our school. I proceeded to give them a suitable date and they said it was fine. They seemed excited that I was going to be able to bring Dr. B to campus. The date actually changed at one point, and we cleared it again with Student Activities and everything was on track.

As the date approached for the event, I gave them the flyer for the event and the Student Activities Office even offered to print the flyers for me, which was a nice surprise given the little money I had to put on this event. My friend in the Student Activities Office printed the flyers for me, and they looked fantastic. We advertised the event as a speaker who was going to talk about *The Struggle Keeping Abortion Safe, Legal and Rare.*"

I had no premonition that there were any problems until one of my professors approached me during class. I quickly learned that the Dean of the school was very concerned about the event. She was in the office when the flyers were being printed and was livid about the event. She immediately called up my program director to complain and, from there, word spread fast about the event and not in a positive light. I had had a night class that evening and a faculty member pulled me aside beforehand and asked me what was happening with the posters. I had no idea what she was talking about.

Apparently it was not "ok" for me to ask a speaker to come and speak to my school. My program director called me manipulative and threatened me with expulsion if Dr. B came to campus. It was at that point that I called the Alliance Defending Freedom, a Christian legal organization that often works with SFLA to defend pro-life groups when their Constitutional rights are threatened. Secretly, I was thrilled I was able to finally call this iconic legal organization in the pro-life movement. I was not happy about the situation I was in but I was happy I got to call ADF!

ADF told me that if it had been a public school and because of the way in which my program director addressed me, she would be fired, the school sued, and we could go on vacation off of the settlement. But since it was a private school I had to comply with their wishes or face expulsion. In the end, Dr. B ended up not coming to my school yet went to nearby Roanoke College through another pro-life group. I helped to advertise his appearance there and was thrilled when we got to meet in person. Because of the "bruhaha," a word my Program Director readily used, Dr. B also spoke at another Medical School in Blacksburg. More students heard his great message because of the conflict.

Struggles and Joys of Being Pro-Life

Choosing to defend those who cannot defend themselves, the voiceless among us, is bittersweet.

It is a struggle sometimes trying to get my own church and peers to see the holocaust happening in our town. Most of my friends even remain apathetic and inactive. Even girls in my Bible study are apathetic about abortion most of the time and do not come out to the abortion facility with me. I have come to understand that each of us has to serve God in different ways, and while I may get angry when my friends fail to act, I have to love them where they are at in their walk.

There are heartbreaks as well. Twice, I was able to bring women to see an ultrasound from the sidewalk of the Bread and Roses abortion facility. Neither women chose life.

And there are joys and victories. In the spring of 2010, my pro-life friends and I single-handedly organized and implemented the 40 Days for Life in Gainesville, Florida - bringing a round-the-clock witness to the Gainesville Planned Parenthood for the first time, ever. During my own participation, when I heard stories and received the daily emails from the national 40 Days for Life Campaign of babies saved, I would share in each victory.

I'm daily reminded that my life path is to run hard for life. I have chosen to do that literally by running 2,012 miles in 2012 in an effort to raise $2,012 for my local pregnancy center (2012milesforlife.blogspot.com). That amounts to about six miles a day!

So much spiritual warfare takes place in the fight to save preborn children. Prayer is so essential to our mission, as is fellowship and courage. I have been to three Students for Life conferences so far, which take place every year around the same time as the anniversary of the *Roe v. Wade* and *Doe v. Bolton* decisions. I always feel like I've entered pro-life heaven. It's like a mission trip, but better. To be surrounded by so much encouragement is priceless. I always come away stronger and with more resolve than when I went.

I will not ever stop speaking up for the preborn and their rights. I believe every life is full of great potential and no matter why or how she entered this world or who her parents may be, she deserves our greatest love and sacrifice.

Caroline Pilgrim is a student at Jefferson College of Health Sciences in Roanoke, Virginia and is looking forward to where God will lead her after graduation in December 2013.

THE POLITICO: BILLY VALENTINE

"The issue on life is not a political issue, nor is it a policy issue, it is a definitional issue. It is a basic core issue that every society needs to answer. The answer that you give to that issue ends up defining which kind of society you have." - Senator Marco Rubio

I was born to dedicate my life to the pro-life movement and to saving the lives of the most innocent and vulnerable in our society. My ancestors ran the Underground Railroad in Indiana. They were Quakers and believed wholeheartedly that slavery was wrong and risked everything to help slaves escape their masters. They were so radical they were even kicked out of their church.

The drive to help those who have no voice continued through the generations in my family. My parents met because of their pro-life work. My dad was the Executive Director of Americans United for Life and my mom worked in the legislative affairs office at the National Right to Life Committee (NRLC). My dad had to fly into Washington, D.C., where my mom worked, to meet with NRLC. She was the first person he met, and he thought she was cute. After their first meeting he called her and asked her out on a date. They were married in 1984 and had five children, three boys and two girls.

With a family history like this, it was really no wonder that I was naturally drawn into the pro-life movement.

Growing up Pro-Life

Abortion was a natural topic of conversation when I was growing up. My parents were very open about it and made it real to me. They weren't afraid to talk about it at a young age. I had a good grasp on what it meant from the time I was very small. Abortion was the tragedy that results in a hurt woman and the end of a human life.

One of my earliest memories was when Bill Clinton ran for president of the United States. I was only five years old at the time but I vividly remember that he was pro-abortion. When he was announced as the winner, I ran and hid under my bed. I thought that as a five-year-old I could still be considered a baby and that he was going to come and get me. Sounds crazy now, but that's how real abortion was to me.

When I was around six or seven years old, I went to a rally with my mom against our Virginia Congressman Jim Moran, who was adamantly pro-abortion and still is. When he walked by me and my mom pointed him out, I literally started shaking; I was petrified of people who thought it was fine, and even sought to promote the so-called right, to kill little babies who weren't even born yet. I thought they may go after little kids like me next.

Since I was little, my mom has basically worked as a full-time volunteer for pro-life candidates and causes in the Northern Virginia area – she's so well-known for her dedication that when an elected official sees her, the first thing they talk about is their pro-life rating. If it isn't perfect, they certainly get an ear full from my mom.

I loved going to my dad's office on Capitol Hill since he did pro-life work on the national stage. He first worked for Senator John East, one of the most pro-life Senators in U.S. history who represented North Carolina in the early 80s. He then worked for Senator Bob Smith from New Hampshire, who was the original chief sponsor of the Partial Birth Abortion Ban Act. My dad spent years working in the U.S. Senate and was very involved with the creation of one piece of legislation that eventually became law - the ban on partial-birth abortion.

Putting Faith into Action

Growing up I saw my mom doing the local grassroots stuff – rallies, phone calls, door-to-door knocking – and, meanwhile, I saw my dad dress up in a suit and tie every day to go to work in the U.S. Senate. Because of my parents, I saw the policy side and the political side of things. I got to learn about all levels of government and activism, which would come in quite handy as I got older and started to become more engaged in the pro-life movement myself. In high school, I ran my pro-life club and in college at Franciscan University of Steubenville, I ran the College Republicans and was active in Students for Life.

Franciscan really stressed putting your faith into action, and I wanted to take that challenge.

One of the things that I didn't really do often with my parents growing up was to go to abortion facilities to pray. Encouraged by my university's teaching to put faith into action, I ended up going to a nearby abortion facility to pray. It was a new experience for me. While there, I would often see sidewalk counselors who tried to talk to the women, and sometimes their partners, who were going into the abortion facility. I decided I wanted to do more than pray. I wanted to be a sidewalk counselor.

When I did sidewalk counseling I usually counseled the men who were going inside the abortion facility with the women. We employed this strategy to our advantage at one particular facility to help save the preborn baby and spare the mother and their partners and families the pain of abortion. This facility didn't allow any cell phones inside – I think they believed that the girl could take the call or read the text of someone who may try to talk her out of the abortion at the last minute. They wanted her to be cut off all contact once she got into the facility. So when the couple would get to the door, the father/boyfriend/husband would take the cell phones and hang out outside of the facility or drive around for awhile. Some of these men would have to travel for blocks to get back to their car since part of our strategy was that 400 students coming from Franciscan to pray every Saturday would take up all the parking spots near the facility, giving us more time to talk to the couple as they walked from their car to the facility.

As a sidewalk counselor, I would have a lot of opportunities to try to talk to the men because of this cell phone rule. I tried to stay as cool as possible and engage them in conversation. Instead of trying to lecture them or spew out scientific facts, I would try to get them comfortable talking in the first place. It makes it harder to ignore a sidewalk counselor if the person you are engaging is comfortable with you instead of automatically labeling you a crazy pro-lifer who just wants to stop the abortion.

I would have conversations with some men who would just break down in tears. To that, my main message would be - "Look, if you go in there and tell your girlfriend that you will support her and be there for her and this baby every step of the way, I guarantee that she'll walk out of there with you."

One thing that was interesting about the sidewalk counseling process at this facility was that there were seminarians and other university students who would come to pray. So sometimes we wouldn't see the fruit of our labor when a woman walked out, but we could still hear about it from some of the other sidewalk counselors we worked with.

While some days were more successful than others, I remember one weekday when I counseled a woman who was pregnant with twins. She had kids at home already who were with her mom, and she said she didn't want to burden her mom with more kids and responsibilities. I told her to go talk to her mom. I was certain her mother, the grandmother of these preborn twins, would see the situation differently and encourage her daughter to have the babies. I saw her on a Thursday and she had the abortion appointment for Saturday. She told me she would think about and if I didn't see her Saturday morning, then she wasn't going to go through with the abortion. She didn't come back on that Saturday, which was awesome.

At Franciscan, we were able to put our faith into action in other ways for these mothers who chose life. Any woman who turned around from the facility and decided to have their baby, as long as they were open to it, we would throw them a baby shower at the university. It was really a beautiful thing and sometimes friendships even developed out of these situations.

The Bubble Zone in Pittsburgh

The city of Pittsburgh, which wasn't far from Franciscan University, introduced bubble zone legislation during my time in college when I was praying outside abortion facilities in that city. Basically bubble zone legislation is aimed at keeping pro-lifers as far away as possible from the abortion facilities so they don't have a chance to persuade a woman away from having an abortion. Most often the legislation is introduced when there has been violence at a facility but that was not the case in Pittsburgh. Yet, the city was under the influence of the abortion facilities and sought to protect them and their profits.

The legislation was introduced on a Tuesday, and it was the front page story the next day in the newspaper. On Thursday morning, just two days after the legislation was introduced, I was outside the local abortion facility in Pittsburgh really early in the morning, around 7am, praying and sidewalk counseling.

As I mentioned before, there was no history of violence outside the facilities in Pittsburgh where I would usually go to pray and sidewalk counsel, but this very morning, myself and the others with me ended up getting severely beaten up by thugs who were waiting for us outside of the facility. The girls were luckily able to run away. A box cutter was held to my neck by one of the women in the group, while my two friends were beaten.

We thought that they were paid – by whom, we don't know. The abortionist claimed to the *Pittsburgh Post-Gazette* that we were trying to stop a girl from going to get an abortion and that these guys were only her cousins and brothers. The supporters of the bubble zone law used this very incident to pass the bill into law. We tried to combat the legislation by starting petitions and getting local people from Pittsburgh to testify at hearings as well as local students. But it wasn't enough.

The law certainly made sidewalk counseling a lot harder. The facility spray-painted the barrier around the prohibited area and the counselors had to specifically ask the girl and her partner permission to come within eight feet of them. But again, that no cell phone rule proved effective on our part.

It made us redouble our efforts. Clearly the abortion facilities were losing business. We saw people circling the facility and when they saw 400 students outside praying; they just didn't go in. They maybe would reschedule, but it gave them another week to think about it.

As my freshman year went on, I did more sidewalk counseling and got more involved in politics too. To be truthful, sidewalk counseling was an emotional and mental drain, and I only did it twice a week.

Working for the Pro-Life Movement

In college, I got involved in the Sam Brownback campaign for President, running Students for Brownback. At the time, Senator Brownback was the leader on life issues in the U.S. Senate. It was an exciting experience being able to organize college students from all across the country. We ended up hiring 40 other Franciscan students as full-time interns in Iowa, and I was able to work as press secretary, even though I really didn't have any press experience. Though we didn't make it past the Ames, Iowa Straw Poll, it was an unforgettable experience.

I then worked for Congressmen Chris Smith in New Jersey on his re-election campaign in 2008. He is the leader for the pro-life cause in the House of Representatives and, so naturally liberals wanted him out of office. I was really honored to be able contribute to his campaign by raising money for his re-election.

In college, I didn't really know what I wanted to do professionally. I majored in legal studies and minored in human life studies. I quickly figured out that I probably wouldn't survive law school, and that I had a calling to be involved politically. So after college I went to Kansas to manage a Congressional race. We lost a 7-way race in the primary. I remember leaving that night, on a Tuesday, and by the following Friday, I was working at the Susan B. Anthony List (SBA List), a major pro-life and political organization based in Washington, D.C. that helps get pro-life candidates elected to office and then uses that leverage to pass pro-life legislation.

I interned for the SBA List off and on starting in 2003 and, seven years later, was happy to make my position there permanent. I remember in 2003 they had a staff meeting to determine if they should allow a guy to intern there, since it's primarily a women's organization. I like to say I broke through the glass ceiling there.

Seeing my parents in the two different worlds of local and national politics really helped prepare me to do my current job, which is to connect policy with politics. But it's constantly changing and shifting gears. A good example was the D.C. Fetal Pain Bill, which was the last pro-life vote we got before August recess in the summer of 2012. I had been working on it for months, and the day after it received a vote, I immediately switched gears to work on a bus tour we were planning later that month to promote pro-life candidates.

I get to do some really great things for the pro-life movement at SBA List. About 75% of what I've been doing is working on defunding the nation's largest provider of abortions, Planned

Parenthood. They have had a "political Teflon" surrounding them for so long– but finally, that has changed.

The pro-life movement has always had a target on Planned Parenthood and the political will to defund them just wasn't there for so many years but Lila Rose's videos have changed all this. She has been able to successfully catch Planned Parenthood on video multiple times aiding child abusers, skirting mandatory reporting laws, abetting child and sex traffickers, and aborting babies just because they are baby girls instead of boys. But the sex trafficking videos in February of 2011 were the turning point.

Planned Parenthood had finally caught on that multiple pimps had visited their clinics asking how to get abortions for young girls who were being sex trafficked, and they called the FBI. Instead of waiting to release the videos at a later time, Lila came out with the damaging videos just when Congress was debating the massive funding resolution, which would continue to fund Planned Parenthood at over $350 million taxpayer dollars a year.

Planned Parenthood, thinking they were getting ahead of the videos, made an error. It was really an exciting time because Planned Parenthood was finally being exposed for what they really were. Lila's videos were everywhere in the media, even running on the evening news while Congress was debating funding the abortion giant. In the end, the government was nearly shut down over funding of Planned Parenthood because President Obama refused to pull taxpayer dollars from one of his favorite groups.

Even though Congress was not able to de-fund Planned Parenthood, it was not a total loss. Following the fight on the national level, several states started taking up legislation to defund

Planned Parenthood from state taxpayer dollars, so the SBA List got involved in state legislation. The SBA List hadn't really been involved in state legislative work previously, but we wanted this fight. So we teamed up with Alliance Defending Freedom to write draft legislation for newly elected Republican legislatures during the 2010 landslide elections.

Governor Jan Brewer of Arizona signed our model legislation into law in May of 2012 which was really exciting for the SBA List since we were there from the beginning and helped put together Arizona De-fund Planned Parenthood rallies, testified before the legislature, and coordinated with state and local pro-life groups across in Arizona. Governor Brewer signed the bill right before my eyes, which was really cool.

Overall, since early 2011, 14 states have taken action to defund Planned Parenthood. Lila Rose and many other pro-life groups have all worked extremely hard on this effort to de-fund Planned Parenthood and being a part of it through the SBA List has been really exciting. Even if we launch an effort in a state that has little chance of passing, we get to say over and over again in any media coverage of the legislation that Planned Parenthood is the nation's largest abortion provider, so it is worth it. So many people just don't know that fact. And even Mitt Romney, when he was running for President, publicly declared his support for de-funding Planned Parenthood.

I want to be a radical like my ancestors who ran the Underground Railroad in Indiana. They fought for and risked their very lives for the defenseless, and I hope I can make them proud.

Billy Valentine is the Director of Policy & Programs at the Susan B. Anthony List and graduated from Franciscan University in Steubenville in 2009.

Kristan Hawkins

THE SIDEWALK HELPER: JULIA PRITCHETT

"We believe so firmly in the humanity of the unborn child that we put ourselves between the child and the abortionist. But we must be armed with knowledge and skill. We have to do the saving through words, actions, right attitude, and prayer." - Joseph Scheidler

The tragic story of Caylee Anthony's death dominated headlines for weeks and then again when her mother, Casey Anthony, was brought to trial for her little girl's murder.

Imagine for just a moment that you knew the time and place when Caylee would be killed. You knew enough details to go to the police and warn them, yet they did not care and made no attempt to prevent her death. What would you do? Would you go to the place at the time of her murder and try to save Caylee?

I think most anyone would try to save Caylee if he could, even if he didn't know how or what he would do when he got there. In the end, he would certainly try to spare the little girl's life.

This is the way I look at sidewalk helping outside of abortion facilities. Because these children are scheduled to die through abortion appointments, I know when and where to be to try to keep that from happening. Whether a woman is casually strolling in or being dragged in by force, I am there to be a peaceful and loving presence with the hope that it will spare her from suffering and her child from death.

From Unaware about Abortion to Aware of My Responsibility

I grew up in Arkansas, not far from Memphis, a southern girl in many ways. When I was young, I had a great attraction to religious sisters and often sat with the ones we had in our parish during Mass. When I was eight, one elderly sister moved back to her convent, and she used her monthly letter privilege to send me a letter. That was the only letter she was allowed to send all month, and she chose me, a child she barely knew. I felt guilty for taking her monthly letter when she had family to write to, but I also felt supremely loved. So, from a young age, I began learning about the importance of human beings, even when those humans feel unimportant or the world thinks and says they are unimportant.

While I was learning these crucial lessons about valuing life when I was little, abortion never came up.

I had never considered myself pro-choice or pro-life, in fact, I'm not sure I really knew what either one meant. Abortion had never forced itself into my consciousness—I was blissfully unaware. When I was a freshman in high school my eyes were opened to just how real abortion was. There was a particular teacher of mine that I looked up to a great deal. She was smart, fair, and talented. Surprisingly, one day this teacher brought up abortion during class. It was not the daily lesson of the class but merely a sidebar in a larger discussion. She spoke about how even many of those people who are opposed to abortion are okay with the rape exception – the exception made for a woman who was raped to choose to abort her child.

Now, my favorite teacher explained this to us by saying that abortion was perfectly legal because the Constitution gave women the right to choose this particular choice. Instantly my heart sank. Had my favorite teacher of all-time just said it was okay to kill babies? Looking back on that moment, I remember the young, impressionable faces of my peers soaking in her words like they were the truth. I'm eternally grateful that God protected me from the same fate of my classmates. Something just clicked inside me.

For a few moments, I sat in internal struggle. I certainly sympathized with women who were raped, but how could that justify killing a baby? In the end, it couldn't. If I believed that abortion was wrong and was the taking of a life at any stage of pregnancy, why would it be okay to take a life because the mother was raped? It is still killing, no matter how a child is conceived.

After class, I literally walked out of the classroom with a new awareness and passion. It was that simple and instant. There were no philosophical arguments to wade through or media influence pushing me in one way or another; just a young and innocent conscience who thought it was a no-brainer that killing babies was never okay.

Since there was no pro-life group at my high school, I made it my mission to get the truth out about abortion to my classmates. I guess I believed that once my peers were forced to think about abortion like I was that it would be just as simple to them as it had been for me.

In a Current Events class I had, we were assigned to bring in a news article every day. So every single day I would bring in an article that would expose abortion for the horrible, scary thing it is. I particularly remember an article about a botched abortion that caused a group of girls in my class to gasp loudly as I read it. I was causing my peers to focus on abortion, even if for just a few minutes every day.

I also participated in the National Pro-Life T-Shirt Week, which asks young people to wear the same pro-life t-shirt every day, for seven days straight. Usually people would start to notice your peculiar wardrobe since you were in class every day with the same clothes on. My A.P. English Literature teacher even joined in and wore a shirt, which meant so much to me. I went to a public school, so any show of pro-life solidarity was appreciated.

Honestly, people thought I was weird. It was hard for them to understand why I cared about abortion more than putting on lip gloss and talking about boys. Some people would tease me and others would go as far as getting a whole classroom against me on the issue of euthanasia. This challenged me to be more relevant to my peers and come up with creative ways to get their attention. I eventually ended up handing out candy that had a pro-life message – I would put 13 sour patch kids in a plastic baggie with a message that told them while they were in class for one period, 13 preborn children would be aborted.

I was so known for my pro-life ways that during my valedictorian speech at our graduation when I said as my closing line "Don't worry, my pro-life antics are just getting started", a big laugh erupted.

My Driving Force

By college, I was passionately pro-life and anxious to continue God's work. Even though growing up I had sworn on my life that I would never attend college in Arkansas, I chose to attend the University of Arkansas since there was no pro-life group there. As soon as I moved to Fayetteville, I started looking for others like myself. During my search I came across a small Knights of

Columbus group on campus. There were two Knights who would go and pray outside of the abortion facility nearby. Although I was a female and they were a male fraternity group, they invited me to pray with them on Saturday mornings outside the facility. Through this experience, I got heavily involved with the local 40 Days for Life campaign as part of the leadership team, which I am still part of to this day. Also, one of the Knights co-founded the Students for Life group on my campus with me during my first semester. Life was good.

40 Days for Life started in 2007 in the small town of College Station, Texas. Pro-lifers wanted to make a difference in their community and show the town that they were going to do everything they could to help mothers and save their preborn children from abortion, so they devised a schedule to pray outside of Planned Parenthood for 40 days and nights, nonstop. The movement mushroomed from there to nearly every state and many other countries as well. Now the National 40 Days for Life organization does 40 Day campaigns twice a year and has mobilized pro-lifers in a way I have never seen in my life. It is work truly inspired by the Holy Spirit. And our group in Fayetteville is composed of people from all walks of life – from Catholics to Protestants, from meat-lovers to vegans, from international students to southerners. We stand outside the local Planned Parenthood and pray and do sidewalk helping when we can.

The first time I prayed during a 40 Days for Life shift was during freshman year, and I was all alone. What I witnessed that day would be my catalyst for becoming a sidewalk helper. Just as that moment in high school was simple and instant, so too would this experience be when I became convinced I needed to learn to sidewalk help. I was standing across the street from the abortion facility, and I saw a young girl who was literally being dragged into the abortion facility by her grandparents. Her shoes scrapped the pavement as they forced her inside. My heart broke into a thousand pieces for her and for her baby. I knew prayer was the most important thing I could do, but I wanted to be able to do more. I wanted to *talk* to her.

For several days I played a cruel "what if" game with myself, asking myself "what if you had called out to her, would she be okay right now?" I never wanted to have to ask myself that question again.

Jumping into the Fire

Because of that experience, I started searching for a pro-life summer internship. I quickly found an internship in the heart of New York City, *the abortion capitol of the U.S.,* that focused on sidewalk helping and helping inside pregnancy resource centers. I barely had any information about what it would be like, where I would live, if I would be paid, etc. But when the organization president called me randomly one day and asked if I was in or out, I just blurted "I'm coming and I'm sure". After hanging up the phone, I sat there in shock for about ten minutes wondering what I had just done.

On my very first day of work, I found myself alone outside of an abortion facility in the Bronx. I was literally walking in a back alley gripping my pro-life literature and searching for women to give it to. I hadn't been trained yet, and I had never sidewalk helped before. Everything was foreign, and I was panicking.

The first couple to walk up to this facility did not speak English. I handed them a Spanish version of the brochure I had with me. I didn't know what else to do, and they ended up walking into the abortion facility as my heart raced. The man came out about two hours later and tried talking to me. I did my best to listen, but I had no idea what he was saying and I just gestured that he follow me to a nearby pregnancy resource center. After following me a ways, he got a little nervous since he did not know where we were going. We had walked half a block when a woman showed up on the sidewalk and asked if I needed a translator. Now, I call that a *God Moment!*

Through the translator, I managed to get the couple to obtain a free ultrasound. The technician spoke Spanish and pointed out the baby's features on the fuzzy picture. She was an ultrasound technician and not a trained helper, so they ended up going back to the abortion facility since they weren't counseled. I was again at a loss. Hours later the couple came out of the facility, walked to the end of the sidewalk, hugged each other, and cried. I silently rejoiced as the couple looked happy and relieved for what I hoped was a decision against abortion.

A few weeks later, I saw this same couple at a different abortion facility. I greeted them and they scurried inside. We were both astounded to see each other, what were the chances?

Then, again, about three weeks after the second sighting, they showed up at a pregnancy resource center where I was assigned to that particular day. I opened the door, and there they were. They were very surprised, as I was myself. We had translators on hand and were able to obtain from them details about their complicated situation. Their situation was so complex that I was instructed to go out in the Bronx streets, find a police officer, and ask him about a "hypothetical situation" and see what he said. I awkwardly did this and never felt so embarrassed. The center director later told me God had made me the godmother of this couple's baby, and I believed her. If you know anything about New York City, you know that only God could have people meet three separate times in three different places like that. That day at the pregnancy center was the last time I saw them, but I believe they ended up keeping their baby once they received help.

The 7-11 Barber Shop

One of my most cherished memories of sidewalk helping happened just outside of Memphis, Tennessee, a few years after coming home from New York. The abortion facility was located in a minority neighborhood, and I have a special place in my heart for minorities since I relate to them - and they to me - really well. A girl pulled up in a beat up car and started looking at me. Once she got out of her car, I was waiting for her and we started talking. In most circumstances I let the woman do most of the talking herself and allow her to share as much as she wants. However, with this woman, Cheye, I felt the Holy Spirit directing me to ask her about her job. Turns out, she was a hair dresser and boy did I need a haircut! I found myself freely offering this information like she was my best friend. She grabbed my ponytail and started going through my hair and promised me she could fix the mess my hair was in. I told her I would come into her shop the next day if she would hold off on her appointment at the abortion facility. It was a deal.

So the next day, I headed deep into Memphis to her hair shop, which turned out to be a barbershop in a rough part of town. There were bars on the windows, and it was attached to a 7-11 gas station. I walked inside and all the customers suddenly stopped talking. White people do not just casually walk into a black barbershop like that in Memphis. Awkward. I headed to the woman's section of the barbershop and all the women there stopped what they were doing and stared at me. Thankfully, I saw Cheye and she got to work on my hair. She put a ton of greasy stuff in my hair, and I was thinking that I had no idea what I had gotten myself into. But she ended up giving me one of the best haircuts I've ever received.

After my haircut, we went to lunch together. We quickly developed a personal friendship and got along great. Not long after our encounter, Cheye discovered that she was not pregnant, but, because of our conversations, she assured me she would not have an abortion even if she did find herself unexpectedly pregnant.

My relationship with Cheye has been incredibly special, and I would never have met her if I was not standing outside that abortion facility. Plus, in this case, I ended up with not only a great friend but also a wonderful hairdresser.

And Deliver Us From Evil

When people find out I do sidewalk helping outside abortion facilities their first reaction almost always is "wow, I don't know if I could do that." There is an automatic feeling people get that makes them feel like they cannot do sidewalk helping. It was a feeling I once had too. Sometimes I still wake up and think that I cannot do it myself.

And, the truth is, I cannot do it myself. If we believe anything we do is of our own merit, we limit ourselves. Every time I stand outside an abortion facility, I am dealing with spiritual warfare and with women in difficult situations. If I did think I could do this on my own, I would be putting myself in a bad, and possibly dangerous, situation. I know I cannot handle this on my own. I trust God, and I know that He is the one doing His work through me. Knowing that God is with me and is watching over me is the only way I am able to do what I do.

Sometimes there are situations that at first terrify me, but again, I have to put my trust in God. It's so funny that I can be alone in my apartment and see a spider and completely freak out, yelling and screaming, but I can be outside an abortion facility and have ten cops get called on me and it does not make me nervous. God gives me the grace and protection I need. He does not send me where He has not gone first. He suffered on the cross first, and so I can trust in Him when I'm bearing my cross.

I have had people yell at me and shout profanities, but it is not demoralizing. People usually are lashing out because of deep-rooted pain within themselves. It makes me want to help people even more because they have been so hurt by abortion. There is a woman in Fayetteville that does pro-life work who cites a particular Bible verse, Matthew 5:12, which is about those who are persecuted on earth having their reward in heaven. If she is hurled an insult of any kind, she says that she wishes the person would have just sent one more insult her way so her reward can be greater in heaven.

The abortion facility where I first prayed during 40 Days for Life in Fayetteville ended up shutting down because the abortionist died of cancer. The *New York Times* obituary of him said that he was a hero because he performed free abortions on victims of Hurricane Katrina. However, this particular doctor used to type up letters and emails to me and send me hate mail to my dorm. It creeps me out to this day thinking about how he could have figured out my name, let alone my address.

People normally seemed shocked when they find out I put my phone number inside every brochure I hand women when I sidewalk help. I have continually been surprised by their shock. In a way it's another simple and instant thing: I came here to help her, so I better mean it. Anyone who has ever sidewalk helped knows that after a while the things you once were timid about are things you think back to and laugh at how silly they were.

For those who have had even the smallest thought of being a sidewalk helper, I would urge you to just be there. Go to the abortion facility and just be there and pray until the Lord breaks your heart for what breaks His. After a while, you'll be on fire to pray *and* help. If you are worried you will not make a difference by being there, well, you won't make a difference just sitting at home. You don't know the effect your presence will have on the women or even the abortion facility workers. More babies have probably been saved by me just standing outside the abortion facility than me actually talking to the mothers. Just like fear tells a woman that she is not ready to be a mom, fear will tell you that you are not ready or good enough to be a sidewalk helper. Don't let fear win, choose courage so that she might choose life.

Julia Pritchett is a senior at the University of Arkansas and is majoring in psychological science. In addition to co-founding her college's Students for Life group, she is a former Students for Life of America Missionary for Life. She plans to do full-time pro-life ministry upon graduation.

THE BIRTHMOTHER: AMANDA LORD

"We look at adoption as a very sacred exchange. It was not done lightly on either side. I would dedicate my life to this child." - Jamie Lee Curtis

I was hoping I could tell the story of when I met my son's dad to my grandchildren, his and mine, I mean. I had a job in Florida delivering barbeque on my moped on a beach. I was on my moped in my bathing suit and he actually cat called me as I drove by. He saw the sign for the company I worked for on the moped and tracked me down. I was only 17 years old when I met him, and we decided we wanted to have a baby when I was 18 and then we were going to get married.

It was an intense romance. He moved into my apartment only three weeks after we started dating, and we had quite the life too. We were pretty much high all the time, doing drugs, going to parties and hitting up raves when they were still cool. I had no idea what a substantive relationship was like and thought that what we had was good enough. I thought he was a great guy too. I really don't know what the idea was behind trying to get pregnant. For me, I think maybe it was that love that every woman pictures about a baby – someone who will always need and love you. For him, maybe it was kind of the same thing.

When I got pregnant, we both got off of the Ecstasy we were doing pretty regularly and sobered up. Thankfully, I wasn't taking any drugs on a regular basis that would have gotten me addicted. As odd as it is to say this, I thought of myself as an "intelligent" drug user who was watched over by a group of guys concerned for my "well-being," as much as doing drugs is meant for any kind of well-being. Once I got off drugs, I was an emotional roller coaster and really struggled with boredom. What did sober people do all day?

Even though my brain was trying to work itself out without drugs, I knew the instant I was pregnant that I was "mom." I was far from being a Christian, so the feeling was not from a religious or moral perspective, and I had no understanding of basic biology to even know that my son was already a tiny human being. I just knew, and that certainly made it easier for me to do the right thing and not use any substance that would be harmful to my baby.

The Abuse Starts

My parents were divorced when I was conceived, and my mom had full custody of me. However, she died when I was five, and I was sent to live with my dad. He was very abusive. I dropped out of high school when I was a senior just so I could go make money and get out of the house and away from my dad.

My fiancé, the father of my preborn baby, suffered from post-traumatic stress disorder after serving in the military and combined with the effects of the abuse I suffered at the hands of my own father and getting off the drugs at the same time, it was like an explosion in our relationship. As soon as I got pregnant, he started abusing me to the point where I was afraid for my safety and that of my preborn baby.

When I was six months pregnant, the abuse got so bad that his own parents told me to get out of the relationship. At that point I escaped into an abuse shelter, which was kind of forced upon me. I had left my fiancé a couple times before believing that I was leaving for good. I've actually read somewhere that the average woman goes back to her abuser anywhere from seven to ten times. It was really the safety of my son that led me to finally leave him for good as I would have probably stayed forever if not for the life of my son.

I had already moved into the abuse shelter when I went into pre-term labor. I was stuck in the hospital for six days, and it was during that time I just fell in love with my preborn baby, who I knew was a little baby boy. I was basically alone with him during those six days in the hospital, and it was wonderful. I was grateful that he was going to be okay, and I could only think of him growing safely inside me.

After I got out of the hospital, I went back to live at the abuse shelter, and they were amazing and even helped me find a good maternity home to move into. They were worried I could go into pre-term labor again and the abuse shelter was not a place to have children.

I had been soul searching for a few years, and the maternity home I moved into was a Christian one. My soul searching had not led me to Christianity at the time, so I was actually pretty ticked off that the home was a Christian one. I knew Christians didn't approve of how I had been living my life, and in my mind they embodied the "holier than thou" attitude and that made me mad. On top of that, I had a lot of anger at God for the death of my Mom and then suffering the abuse at the hands of my Dad so moving into a Christian maternity home was not a great thing in my mind.

Adoption?

When a new woman entered the maternity home, it was standard procedure to have a review meeting with the home director and mother. During my review, the director asked me the standard questions about myself, my intentions, my baby, etc. She also asked me if I had ever considered adoption, and I got really angry, like spewing venom angry. I had always known that I was going to parent my son, and I felt my parenting skills were being questioned, which they probably should have been. I took the director's question as a personal attack, an attack against my love for him. Even if I wasn't ready to parent my son, I loved him so much and was ready to do whatever I needed to do. Yet, despite the anger, I began to think about placing my son with an adoptive family.

In the end, it came down to it not being about me, but about my son. When I was in the hospital during the pre-term labor, I was stuck watching crappy daytime television and there was a commercial that always came on with the Alicia Keys song in it, "If I Ain't Got You," which basically said the world means nothing if I don't have the person I love. What would my world look like if I didn't have my son? Or, more importantly maybe, what would my son's world look like if I kept him and was not able to give him the basic necessities of life?

I made a pros and cons list about placing him for adoption, and I included what I wanted his parents to be able to provide for him. Even though I wasn't a Christian, I wanted his parents to be Christian. I knew Christians had some kind of weird morality that I wanted for my son. I also wanted them to be hippie, outdoorsy, and have a non-traditional lifestyle.

When I was considering adoption, I saw about 30-40 *profiles* which were the letters from families who wanted to adopt to potential birth moms. Some were cheesy, but I landed on one couple, pretty much because they loved to sail. Growing up in Florida, that was important to me for some reason. This particular couple had not tried the in-vitro fertilization route or any other outside method of achieving pregnancy other than naturally. Adoption was not a last ditch effort for them, and they were open to adopting more kids, which was important because I didn't want my son to be an only child.

I made up my mind to place my son for adoption, and I had to sign a preliminary document that stated that I "fully intend" to relinquish my parental rights, which basically gave my son's adoptive parents a sense of stability. I hadn't met them before I gave birth, but I had talked to them over the phone, and they were awesome. Now that I'm in the pro-life movement, I realize that they did everything right when it came to the adoption. They wanted to know all about me, even what I thought my son's name should be. They were funny and warm people. Even though they didn't end up selecting my suggestion for my son's name, Sage Addison; I still think they are awesome. He would have grown up with dreadlocks. So he is very lucky!

I told my son's birth father over e-mail that I was placing my son for adoption, and I never saw a response because I blocked his name immediately. I just wanted that chapter of my life to close.

I went into labor and gave birth to a beautiful boy who weighed seven pounds and four ounces. I had already fallen in love with him, but, at that moment, it was the happiest moment of my life. I couldn't imagine happiness like that.

I was in the hospital for two and a half days, and then I relinquished my parental rights for good after I got to meet his adoptive parents. I ended up putting my son in the custody of ladies at the maternity home for the first day or so after his birth, because I didn't want to give into my temptations of walking out of the hospital with him.

The hospital was a turning point for me. My pregnancy was over, my son was born, and I wanted to say goodbye to him and do it my way, which was saying goodbye alone. I had this horrible fear of having to place him in the arms of his adoptive parents. At the time I wasn't ready, but, if I could go back, I would have done it.

If my son tries to search for me when he is of age, that would be amazing. His adoptive mom and I discussed this briefly, and we agreed that if he wanted to meet me, I would love to meet him, as long as it was not an act of rebellion.

Converting to Christianity

When I was living in the maternity home, I debated Christianity with anyone who would listen...or anyone forced to listen. During these debates, I would often begin screaming at the director. I remember yelling at her and seeing all the other women at the home staring at us wondering what was happening.

While at the maternity home, I went to Christian counseling and the counselor put to shame all my stereotypes about Christians. She had told me the sins she committed as a Christian, and I was shocked. I had always been searching for spirituality and what plagued me the most about Christianity was the love that God has for us. I knew I was flawed; I wasn't a good human being.

My conversion happened, literally, at the moment I was giving birth to my son. In the agony of labor, while pushing my son to join this world knowing that I was giving him to another family, I understood at that moment what it meant to love someone so much to give him up. I finally understood what Christians had meant when they said that God loved his son so much that He gave him up, and I loved my son so much that I was going to give him up. God loved me intensely, and He gave up his only son for me and for my sins. What an incredible kind of love.

I didn't become a Christian at that exact point but it was certainly an epiphany and moment of clarity in my soul searching. It was only a couple months later I became an "official" Christian. In the end, I think that it always came back to that moment with my son. No matter what I've done or what I will do; I am loved.

Now, my walk with Christ had turned me into a nerd because I read a lot of apologetics books. I have learned that I truly walk in grace, grace towards others and especially reminding myself daily of God's grace towards me. I have to trust that God has taken care of my son. It's difficult to think about sometimes, that my son is out there without me, but I just need to let it go and trust that God is taking care of him.

From the Moped to the Pro-Life Movement

After I had my son, I continued to live at the maternity home for a few months and then moved around a bunch. I got my GED while eight months pregnant, but I wanted to go to college so I moved to Fort Worth, Texas and went to school for sociology.

While living in Texas, I got it in my head that I wanted to become a missionary and do pro-life work full-time. A close friend of mine Kortney Blythe posted on her MySpace page about an opportunity to do pro-life missionary work in California with Survivors of the Abortion Holocaust. I applied, got the job, and picked up and moved. At Survivors, we went around college campuses and educated students on abortion and that they are survivors of the American holocaust: abortion. One-third of the generation born after 1972 has been wiped out because of legal abortion, and the majority of these students had no idea they were survivors. During my time with Survivors, I went to 600 college and high school campuses.

Two years later, Kortney moved back to the East Coast to work for the American Life League (ALL) right outside of Washington, D.C., and I moved there as well to take care of my dad who was diagnosed with cancer. I eventually ended up working for ALL with Kortney. Through our work with ALL, we heard about Students for Life of America, and we both went to work for that organization.

Kortney got married and became pregnant after she started at SFLA, but, in October 2011, Kortney, her preborn baby Sophy, and another SFLA team member, Jon Scharfenberger, were killed in a head on crash as they were driving back from an SFLA conference in Georgia.

I've worked for SFLA for two years. I'm the Field and Social Media Coordinator, so I work with all the student groups and train them in effective pro-life activism. I give adoption talks as well.

In 10 years, I hope that I won't have to be working in the pro-life movement because we will have abolished abortion. But no matter what, I think I will always be doing some kind of pro-life work and helping women who are pregnant and their babies. I'd like to have kids of my own one day, but I would also love to adopt. I want to be able to do something special for a birth mom and give something to her because she is placing her child with me.

I think those of us in the pro-life movement need to be honest about abortion and the harm it causes to both mother and child, but I also think we need to be honest about adoption too. Women need to know the truth. Adoption is really hard at first. I couldn't imagine doing anything more difficult than that. We need to be honest with women and help them to know the adoption is for their baby and not about themselves. And if a woman is so abortion-minded and is in a crisis and can only think about herself, adoption is such a better decision than abortion for her physically, emotionally, and spiritually.

I'm not going to lie; I do get sad, and I do miss my son. But in the end, my son is alive, and I have faith that he is happy and flourishing. With abortion, all you can think of is all you've done wrong, and, with adoption, all you think of is what you've done right, which is your baby.

Amanda Lord was the Field and Social Media Coordinator at Students for Life of America. In Spring 2013, she is starting school to become an ultrasound technician.

THE UN-EXPECTING PRO-LIFE ACTIVIST: STEVE MACIAS

"People grow through experience if they meet life honestly and courageously. This is how character is built." – Eleanor Roosevelt

I never had any intention whatsoever to get involved in the pro-life movement. Yes, I was pro-life, but not someone who was defined by that view or who got actively involved in protecting the preborn. I was a conservative activist in California *(yes, we do exist)* who managed to get in a lot of hot water because I stood up for my beliefs. Here is my story.

Family and Faith

My mom was only 15 years old when she became pregnant with me, and my dad was 18. When she got pregnant with me, she was kicked out of her parents' house and had to move in with my dad's family. They were married at a courthouse a month before I was born. It was either that or never have relationships with their parents again. Amazingly enough, 22 years later, I have a younger sister and brother, and my parents are still together.

I grew up in Sacramento, California and never really had any type of religious upbringing. My dad's family was Catholic, but he had left the Church long before I was born. Both my parents belonged to labor unions, so their thinking was really shaped by the Democratic National Party, which ironically enough is in large part opposed to the Christian worldview. Most everything from the Christian work ethic to the sanctity of life are opposed by the Democratic Party agenda.

When I was 17, my Aunt Marie gave me tickets to a rock concert for my birthday. But she was sneaky – the rock concert was actually a Christian youth conference with a concert at the end. Skeptical as I was, I wasn't upset. I knew what I believed, what I had been taught in my non-religious household, and it definitely wasn't this Christianity stuff.

However, God had a plan for me at that rock concert. The three-day youth conference started to work on my heart and began to tear down those lies that I held so close. On the second day, there was an altar call where everyone, who already hadn't, was invited to publicly acknowledge that they wanted a personal relationship with Jesus Christ. I wanted that, and it was then that I gave my life to Christ. I went to the rock concert a non-believer and came back a Christian.

It was hard for my parents to accept at first because the church I eventually joined was similar to the concert – evangelical and edgy – and they thought I was getting brainwashed going to youth group and church several times a week. They eventually came around, accepting that this wasn't some fad, even though they still aren't Christians.

Changing the World

As an aspiring conservative activist in California, I led the College Republicans on the Sacramento City College campus, and we had this grand idea to take over our student government with Republicans. So we launched a campaign to take all the student government seats in order to implement our ideas. Our student government was not very active, something we didn't know that at that time. We all filed for student government seats only to discover that most of us were running for uncontested seats. No one had even registered to run for student body president. Our plan would work!

You could register for multiple seats so we all thought we would register for basic Senate seats. About six or seven of us became senators and did what we were supposed to do - go to meetings, learn the system, etc. - for a couple semesters. After a year, we all figured we could be a lot more impactful.

We learned that our student newspaper would print out the biographies of people running for office – the larger the office, the more space you would get in the paper. Being the evangelical Christian and Republican activist I am, I decided to put a Gospel message inside of my biography, which would take up a whole page, as I ran for student body president. As I filled out the paperwork, I wondered if including the Gospel would hurt my run for this position. However, not only did my Gospel message rock, but I had no opposition. God had opened all the doors and made me the new student body president. I was thrilled.

Deepening my Pro-Life Convictions

That was an exciting time for me, but things were about to change. That spring, shortly after being accepted as student body president, I was in the student body office and got a phone call that there was a group on campus handing out controversial literature and that I needed to take a look at it.

I checked it out and found out that they were pro-life protestors handing out brochures about abortion. They asked me if I was a Christian and how I felt about abortion. I told them that I was a

Christian and abortion was an important issue. I continued on and said that we should all vote pro-life and that it should be a litmus test for Republican candidates. But that was the wrong answer.

They asked what I was doing to save the babies. I told them I was into politics and was the student body president. They took that to mean that I could get stuff done on campus, so they asked to meet with me.

They met with me not long after and showed me a video of an abortion being performed. You know what abortion is, but you don't see what it does. You know it's wrong, but seeing it actually happening is another thing. It was hard to watch. After watching the video, I was convinced I had to do something, anything, and I asked what I needed to do.

They were obviously prepared for that question and told me they wanted to do a Genocide Awareness Project display on campus. This project, known as GAP, is huge. It is a photo mural of four panels behind a barricade that shows graphic pictures of an aborted fetus throughout its development and compares it to genocide throughout history – the Holocaust and American slavery. The display shows how genocide dehumanized these "unpopular" people in history based on gender, ethnicity or skin color and links it directly to the dehumanization of the preborn baby.

So what did I need to do? They wanted the student government to sponsor the GAP, so they could bring it to my campus. I agreed.

This would be the first time a student government had ever sponsored the GAP on a college campus. We looked at the calendar and decided on "Constitution Day" in early September which was established by President George W. Bush. All public institutions of higher learning had to have a day where they talked about voter registration and the Constitution, and we thought that fit perfectly.

As the student body president, I had to go through the steps the school required to bring such a display to campus. I put it on our agenda and brought it before the Board, who voted to allow it. I and my fellow conservative activists did it all by the book, and it was officially sponsored by the student government.

Into the Fire

When Constitution Day came and the GAP display was set up on campus, I went to class as usual, but soon after class started, my phone started ringing off the hook. I was immediately pulled into a meeting with all the higher ups on campus – the administration, campus police etc. – who breathlessly proclaimed that the display was dangerous and demanded to know how I could allow it on campus.

They were really upset and begged me to tell them that the student government was not the sponsor of the display. Our name was on the project, so what could I say? The Vice President of Student Services pulled me out into the hallway. He told me I was making an ass out of him. He said I was making a huge mistake and that I needed to tell them to take down the display.

"Mr. Poindexter, I can't do that," I said calmly, even though inside I was trembling.

Right after that meeting I ran down to the display and told the pro-lifers that the school wanted them to take down the display. They had obviously been through this before and were not worried. They told me that the school can't tell them to take it down. Hey, I believed them.

I headed over to our student government office, and it was mayhem. The student government had never sponsored something like this, and it didn't conform to the radically left atmosphere of the institution.

The phones were ringing, people were lining up outside. There were even women crying who had seen the display and were affected by what they had witnessed. We had tons of people complaining about it. The GAP event didn't go unnoticed by anyone on campus.

To get into our student government office, I had to weave through the crowd of people. The campus advisor met with me privately in there and told me that there had been a bomb threat called in to the office. A bomb threat? It was a storm on campus, and I was right in the middle of it.

I went home and tried to put the event behind me. Meanwhile, the email listserv for the school was on fire – any email sent to this listserv by a student, professor, or administrator went to the all people in the school, administration and staff included – as teachers were emailing back and forth saying that they were appalled that the school allowed this display on campus.

The next day, the student newspaper's website had all these blurbs about the display and videos of people's responses. But the display had been originally approved for two days, so we had another 6 hours of GAP planned for the campus.

I was out there the second day for part of the GAP but didn't want to be too associated with the display because I was already in a lot of trouble. But students volunteering with the display were telling me amazing stories nevertheless.

They had two women approach them who were pregnant and had come up to the people at the display saying they had decided to keep their babies. They had women on campus say that they had repented from their abortions and accepted Christ because they saw the display. They had women say that they could never choose abortion because they had seen the display. It inspired a lot of good dialogue.

The day after the GAP finished, I had been asked to speak at a faculty appreciation type of luncheon. As I got up to the podium to speak, I could feel the darts being thrown at me mentally as the attendees thought that this is the kid that brought that disgusting display to campus.

But then the day got even better. As I left the faculty event, I saw that the Queer-Straight Alliance, along with the Atheist Free Thinkers Club, had set up a booth in the quad in the middle of campus whose sole purpose was trying to recall me as student body president. Not afraid of controversy, I walked over to see what was going on.

In middle of the now-substantial crowd, a young lesbian jumped up on the table and yelled that "in this office over here *(here being the student body office)* there is a fascist bigot named Steven Macias who wants to force his anti-choice views onto the entire student body. He's a Christian zealot who wants nothing but the stoning of women who have had abortions and doesn't want to offer any hope even to those who have been raped. He was out here saying that women who got raped deserve it."

I wasn't even out there during the GAP display when they were doing the witnessing. I was out there at times, in between classes, but never actually participated in the display. So I went up to her and introduced myself. She had no idea I was the person she was talking about. I tried to explain to her my intentions in hosting the display, but she wouldn't listen. It wasn't a nice conservation.

The Recall Election

Outspoken liberal members of the student body, like that girl who was spreading lies about me by yelling at the top of her lungs on campus, and the atheist group, wanted me recalled from office.

There were specific rules they needed to follow, and they were required to collect something like 4,000 to 5,000 signatures. They conducted a huge public relations campaign against me in the newspaper but couldn't get the number of signatures they needed.

Nevertheless, the Student Services Office announced that there would be a recall election. There are regulations in the student government on how to do this and the school basically broke every single one of them. They ignored the rules.

At that point, I called the Alliance Defense Fund (ADF), now called Alliance Defending Freedom, a great legal organization that helps support pro-life causes and defend First Amendment rights. ADF fired off a letter to the school saying that they were required to follow their own rules. The school refused to release the number of signatures the recall petition had actually garnered and the validity of them. However, they did agree to one of their rules which was to make sure to hold the recall election at least two weeks after signatures were collected to give me time to prepare a counter campaign.

So I prepared. I launched my own campaign – I drew in every conservative leader on campus, sent out emails, and handed out around 15,000 pieces of literature.

Then the recall election was finally held. However, the day after the election, the school said there had been an "abnormality" in the results, and they wouldn't be releasing the final numbers and would hold another recall election!

What I figured was that we won and that had been the abnormality. ADF helped me again and sent more letters to the school saying that they were still not following their own policies. Their letters helped to delay the second recall election.

But now there was another problem. Even though the Republican members originally had the majority of the student government, after the first recall election, we ended up losing our majority. The leftists took over some of the seats Republicans previously held, and they were upset that the school wasn't doing enough to remove me as president of the student body. So, they proposed and passed their own student government resolution no longer recognizing me as student body president and removing my authority over any meetings or expenditures. Basically, they recalled me without an election.

For a third time, ADF launched further legal action and an article was published that was circulated widely among the blogosphere. My story garnered national attention, and I went on Michael Medved's nationally syndicated radio show as well as other shows. I was so excited to be able to get the word out about my unjust situation.

The school eventually issued an apology to me and removed the resolution that the liberal student government had passed and reinstated me as student body president. Finally, a letter from the president of the college reiterated their apology and said that free speech was always welcome on campus.

It had been a tough situation. Even my parents, who were not pro-life, were encouraging me to just do what the school wanted me to do, apologize for the display and move on.

But with the backing of my friends and ADF, I really wanted to show the other students at my school that they didn't have to give in to every attack on their freedom.

After the episode at my school, I was asked to go speak at an ADF event in Arizona and even got to speak on a panel on academic freedom at the Conservative Political Action Conference (CPAC) in front of thousands of attendees in 2010 in Washington, D.C. That is where I met Kristan Hawkins of Students for Life of America, and once I finished the semester, I got a job with SFLA.

I went to Liberty University online for two semesters, but I still haven't graduated college. I know that working in the pro-life movement right now is more important. My goal is to be a pastor, but I have to wait until I turn 30 in my denomination, so I figure that means I have about eight years to end abortion.

Suppressing Freedom Backfires

Six months prior to the recall, I had no interest in pro-life work and wasn't even involved in pro-life activities. But afterwards, I went on to start 50 pro-life groups in California and Arizona. I have spoken at dozens of conferences and met thousands of students. What the abortion supporters on campus tried to suppress with their recall really backfired against them. By trying to get rid of me, they actually pushed me to become a passionate leader in the pro-life community.

Steve Macias is now the executive director of Cherish California's Children, a non-profit founded in 2001 to financially support the efforts of existing life-affirming organizations in California. Cherish also produces various Christian leadership materials for advancing the intellectual integrity of the pro-life movement.

THE PREGNANT STUDENT: CHAUNIE BRUSIE

"It is not until you become a mother that your judgment slowly turns to compassion and understanding." - Erma Bombeck

Staring down at those two tiny blue lines, illuminated by the fluorescent light of my student apartment, with my boyfriend motionless in the corner, I screamed—a sound so desperate and gut wrenching that felt like it couldn't possibly be coming from me.

In that instant, looking down at the two lines that forever changed my life, I forgot what I had been taught about abortion. I forgot what I had believed my entire life. I forgot everything that I had worked so hard for as a pro-life student activist.

Instead, all I felt was fear. Complete, overwhelming, and debilitating fear about what those two lines meant.

No one would ever have to know, I thought to myself. *No one would ever have to find out.*

The Beginning

Growing up as a pro-life Catholic, I was immersed early into the pro-life movement. I felt passionate about advocating against abortion, so, when I transferred to a public school in 10th grade and learned that—lo and behold—not everyone believed what I believed, I started working more actively in the movement. I founded my high school's first pro-life club, raised money to take our group to the March for Life, volunteered at a pregnancy help center, and participated in sidewalk counseling.

I continued my activism when I went to college at Saginaw Valley State University in Michigan, where I, again, founded my school's first pro-life group. Typical of many pro-life groups, we were small but mighty and continued the efforts I had started in high school—volunteering, posting flyers on campus, and raising awareness through events and discussion tables with other students.

But I felt that our efforts were going nowhere; instead of reaching out, I felt that our group was alienating. Instead of working together towards solutions, I felt animosity towards our group. And above all, instead of helping the very women who were most likely to choose abortion, I felt that we were pushing them away.

Then one day, I saw an ad for Feminists for Life, a pro-life, pro-woman organization that advocates for resources for pregnant and parenting students. I was blown away by their message of ending abortion by advocating for the practical support and resources that pregnant women need and immediately applied for an internship with them. After an incredible summer internship with the organization, I returned to school in the fall, fired up to help pregnant and parenting students on campus. But I never expected to become one.

What If?

On a weekend off from school at the start of our senior year, Ben, my boyfriend of four years, and I stopped off for a picnic in the park with my siblings. Nibbling on what should have been a delicious pumpkin spice donut, I found myself fighting waves of nausea. When Ben asked me if I was all right, I laughed it off, chalking my upset stomach up to junk food. But later that night, as we headed back to school, I hesitantly turned to Ben and told him that my period was a little late.

"How late?" he asked.

I felt the blood drain from my face. "Um, well, it's just a little late...let me think, I had it in August, so it's only...(pause)...three weeks late."

Ben continued driving in silence, his face emotionless. That night, I decided to take a pregnancy test.

I found myself drinking a water bottle as Ben and I sped to Rite-Aid shortly after midnight. I browsed the selection of pregnancy tests (*Should I get the E.P.T. or chance the off-brand? Did I want one test or two?*) while Ben pretended to examine batteries in the next aisle. As we checked out, I found myself staring at the young cashier, memorizing a face I knew I would never forget, wondering how he could possibly ring us up so calmly when my life could be changing forever.

When I got home, I dutifully peed in a cup and brought the test out to the kitchen, where Ben waited. I paused, holding the test over the edge, hoping, praying that I could prevent my life from crashing around me for just a moment longer.

I held my breath and dipped the test. *What if....?*

Before the test was even done, I saw them.

Two tiny blue lines innocently aligned in the form of a presumptuous "plus" sign.

I tore open the second pregnancy test and dunked it. Positive again.

I was 21, unmarried, a student in my senior year of college, and still taking my laundry home to my parents every weekend. And now, I was a mother. "What if" quickly became "what now?

Pregnant on Campus

After taking my home pregnancy test, in a state of desperation and denial, I turned to the first place I thought of—my college Campus Health Center. At the center, I took yet another test and waited for the result. When the Director of the Center called me into her office, there was no denying it—I was pregnant.

Fighting back panic, I tried to calmly discuss my options with the Director. Was there maternity coverage in the student insurance? Could I stay under my parents' insurance if I got married? Where could I go for help? Could she recommend a good doctor in the area?

The Director of a college Campus Health Center somehow had no answers for me as a pregnant student. Instead of helping me talk through my options or directing me to resources, she turned the tables on me and asked me how I would tell my parents.

In answer to her, I did what any pregnant, Catholic girl would do— I burst into tears. While I sat sobbing uncontrollably in her chair, more scared and confused than when I had arrived, she examined her chart in silence.

After about a minute or two, she stood up and walked out on me. As she closed the door, she said, "I have other patients to see, but you can stay in here if you want."

Advocating for Change

I was devastated by the lack of support and resources available to me as a pregnant student. Fortunately for me, I was able to find support through my family, who celebrated a new life without judgment or condemnation and encouraged me that I could succeed, as well as my boyfriend, who quickly became my fiancé, and then over Christmas break, my husband.

Looking back to the night I found out I was pregnant, I am very honest when I say that abortion absolutely crossed my mind. Even after all that I knew about abortion, even after all that I had advocated for as a pro-lifer, the fear and shame I felt with my pregnancy overwhelmed everything else.

My baby didn't feel real to me yet; the only thing that felt real was the fact that my life as I knew it was now over. I thought about how much I desperately just wanted things to back to normal and how abortion really seemed like it could do that for me.

I never understood how a woman could consider abortion until it was me. The truth is that the fear, panic, and shock clouds a woman's mind and makes it impossible to think clearly. I knew the horror of abortion and yet I *still* wanted to believe that there could be an easy way out. Abortion preys on that vulnerability of women and traps them into thinking it's a quick fix.

When you think about a woman in that state of desperation and then consider the lack of resources and support that exist for her, is it any wonder that the majority of abortions are occurring in college-aged women?

I am sure I was not the first pregnant student to walk into my college health center. So why didn't my school have the resources or trained staff to handle the needs of a pregnant woman? As I would soon find out, colleges across the nation are not equipped with the resources that pregnant and parenting students need. Even more alarming, schools that *do* have resources in place fail to advertise them to the students that need them most.

I knew something needed to change. Vowing that no pregnant woman would ever be left alone and in tears again, I set out to change my campus.

Together, my club members and I decided to change the focus of our pro-life group. We changed the name of our club to S.U.P.P.O.R.T (Supporting Unplanned Pregnancies and Organizing Resources Together) and set out to do just that—support pregnant and parenting students.

One by one, my pregnant belly and I marched into offices on campus and demanded support for pregnant and parenting students. With a looming due date, we worked hard to create change that would last longer than my skinny jeans.

By the close of the year, I had worked with the Director of Counseling and Health Services to completely change the way pregnant students were treated. Together, we designed a comprehensive pregnant and parenting services page for the school's website with answers to all of the questions I had once asked and more. Women who now came into the Campus Health Center for pregnancy testing were automatically offered resources and one-on-one guidance from the counseling center. The Campus Health Center was re-designed to protect a woman's privacy, and they even hired a new Health Director. Other offices on campus got on board too—I convinced the Director of Financial Aid to train his staff on guidelines pertaining to pregnant women. For instance, did you know that a pregnant woman can claim her preborn child as a dependent, potentially qualifying her for increased financial aid?

We also worked with Feminists for Life to host the nation's first-ever Rally for Resources, a resource fair designed just for pregnant and parenting students. The fair was a huge success—I didn't even know how many pregnant and parenting students existed at our school until we started talking about the issues. As an added bonus, our fair featured free massages and manicures—perfect for hardworking pregnant students!

Becoming a Mother

While I was proud of everything I had accomplished on campus for other students like me, I struggled immensely with accepting my pregnancy. It may sound old-fashioned now, but Ben and I really did want to wait until we were married to have sex. It felt like we fought against it–and then failed.

Which is how I came to view my whole start into motherhood—as a failure.

In my eyes, with my own spiritual beliefs and background, I had *sinned.* I had done something I wasn't supposed to do, and now, I was pregnant as a result. How on earth could I possibly be excited about it? How could I even begin to think that my baby was anything but a consequence of my bad behavior?

I felt trapped in a little cloud of guilty darkness for the first half of my pregnancy. I couldn't see a way out. I couldn't see how my baby, conceived out of a "bad" thing, could possibly be a "good" thing. Surely, she would be emotionally messed up, marked by my sin, scarred by a marriage that started badly. Surely, I would never love her the way a "real" mother would–the kind that planned for a baby, and surprised her husband sweetly with the positive pregnancy test and shopped excitedly for nursery decorations.

I wanted to be a "real" mother. The kind that fell in love with her baby and felt happiness, not fear, with those first little flutters in my belly. But first, I needed to accept my pregnancy. For me, that took months of prayer.

And one night, it finally happened.

After a long day of classes, work, disappointments, and wedding stress, I sat curled up on our raspberry-cream colored hand-me-down couch. And for the first time in my life, I felt I very clearly was given an answer: **My baby was not a punishment.**

The moment I felt those words reverberate within me, I felt so relieved. I felt peace. I realized that on some level deep down, I was waiting for the other shoe to drop. I had been hiding in the shadows, cringing in shame, just waiting for God to strike me down with spite.

And suddenly, I realized I had it completely wrong. God didn't punish me with a baby. Sure, maybe I hadn't done everything perfectly, but He wasn't about to give up on me so easily. I felt, with a sudden realization of happiness, that God had sent us our baby as an opportunity to learn the truth about love.

Because, after all, what else provides a faster lesson in true and selfless love than a baby?

It took a long time for me to come to terms with my pregnancy. For me, prayer and a faith in God were key. I know everyone is different, but I know I can't be alone in the conflicting feelings of guilt and shame and the need to feel like it's ok to be happy about a "surprise" baby.

And on May 17, at 4:51 p.m., after fourteen hours of labor, the moment I feared so much became laughable as I gazed down at the most beautiful sight in the entire world: my daughter. Holding my baby girl, my heart sighed in recognition. She was both a part of me and so completely her own, and I fell completely head over heels in love.

Life After an Unplanned Pregnancy

After our daughter was born, it was a difficult first year, with Ben finishing up school, moving, and me working nights as a nurse. I don't want to downplay any of the challenges that having a baby unexpectedly can bring (the whole lack of sleep *is* kind of a big deal), but I was also thrilled to discover the unexpected ways she changed my life for the better.

Aside from the obvious fact that she was the most perfect child that ever existed, having my daughter actually propelled me to live all of my dreams. Because of my experience with her, I was able to land a dream job working for Feminists for Life, traveling and speaking about supporting pregnant and parenting students. I've been able to connect with other young moms out there and create a support network of amazing women who are working so hard to raise their children while living their lives as students, mothers, and professionals. And I've been inspired by all their stories to live my own dream of becoming a writer—I just signed a contract for my first book!

And now, as a 26-year-old mother of three, (we welcomed our second daughter in May 2010, and our son in July 2012) the blessings have continued. I truly believe that I am a better person for having my daughter—I am more patient and more willing to try new things. I've thrown away my checklist for life (most of it, anyways) and have learned to live in the moment and accept God's plans, instead of always trying to make my own. I know that life is fleeting and precious and I work hard, even between the tantrums and tears, to find joy in every day.

I love the mother that I am now, and I am happy to say that I found the answer to the "what if" question I asked that night four years ago. Her name is Ada Marie.

Chaunie Brusie is a writer, labor and delivery nurse, speaker, and advocate for young mothers. She blogs about life as a young mom of three at www.tinybluelines.com. Her book on young motherhood and unplanned pregnancy is due in May 2014 through Ave Maria Press.

THE SUPPORT SYSTEM: MEGHAN REDMOND

"The first question which the priest and the Levite asked was: 'If I stop to help this man, what will happen to me?' But... the good Samaritan reversed the question: 'If I do not stop to help this man, what will happen to him'?"
- Martin Luther King, Jr.

I booted up my computer after class to check my email. The fall semester had just started, and I was really busy with classes and working with Students for Life of America to get our new pro-life group under way.

I pulled up the inbox for the Sacramento State Students for Life group and my heart alternatively constricted with concern and expanded with compassion. The email read:

"Hi – my name is Jessica. I had an abortion and I met you guys at your table the other day. I'd like to get involved and help other girls so they don't make the same mistake I did."

I remembered Jessica. She was with a couple other girls who came by my table and took some of our pro-life information. She was a pretty, African American girl who was just starting her junior year. What I couldn't see was the pain she was hiding from her abortion, or rather, abortions. I came to find out she had had two of them.

She had just had the last abortion a few months earlier and her life was spiraling out of control. She was barely holding it together. Like most women, she was very good at outwardly portraying a happy girl yet she was crumbling on the inside. She was working two jobs and going to school, and her relationship with the father of her aborted child had just broken up, so it was a very difficult time for her.

What if the pro-life group had been at campus a year before? Could we have prevented that abortion? I tried not to dwell on those questions though as my thoughts and prayers were consumed with Jessica. A girl faced with an unplanned pregnancy needs a supportive hand, someone to be there for her and encourage her during her pregnancy. A mother knows she has a child growing inside her, but she needs support.

Jessica was very unique in that she wanted to face her regret about her abortions and confront the pain head on. Most women her age who have had abortions do not do that. In fact, many post-abortive women take years to even begin to deal with the ramifications of the choice to abort their child.

But Jessica was different. She and I formed a close friendship and, after much prayer, I helped get Jessica in contact with Rachel's Vineyard, a program that holds three-day healing retreats for women who have had abortions. Jessica went and was the youngest girl there. All the other women were so impressed with her openness and willingness to heal. She's a very special woman with a sensitive conscience.

When I picked her up from the retreat, immediately I recognized in her a totally different person. She was beaming and happy. After the retreat, she became an officer in our pro-life group, started praying at abortion facilities, and committed herself to chastity. She wrote an essay for school about her abortions, spoke at local 40 Days for Life events, and helped other women who had abortions.

But a year later Jessica was facing a situation she had hoped and prayed would not happen again; she was unexpectedly pregnant for a third time.

Passionately Pro-Life

Most pro-lifers would probably call themselves "passionate," so, in that sense, I'm no different than my peers who see abortion as the greatest genocide in modern history and want to end it. I am one of eight children who grew up in a Catholic family with pro-life values. When I was in high school, I attended pro-life rallies and conferences. A woman who survived an attempted abortion, Gianna Jessen, solidified my pro-life views. Gianna's story is so riveting that there is no denying that abortion is truly a murderous act and the taking of a human life. Once you hear her and others like her speak, there is no other way to see abortion.

When I entered college at Sacramento State, I immediately saw that there was a severe lack of knowledge of prenatal development and wanted to start a pro-life group to help draw awareness to how the littlest among us develop in the womb. I wanted to convert the world (who doesn't?), so I contacted SFLA for some tips and starter materials, found a few others like myself, and started tabling, handing out pro-life magazines, and putting pro-life flyers around campus.

I had no idea what I was getting myself into. I would give away pro-life magazines with pictures of developing preborn babies and articles on abortion, but at least 9 out of every 10 magazines people took ended up in the trash. But what if that one magazine that avoided the garbage was read or was left in the library where a pregnant woman glanced at it? As it is with a lot of work in the pro-life movement, most of the time we don't see the fruit of our labors and have no idea the lives we may have saved. But for that alone, our work is worth it. This is our calling and our vocation, and we try our best.

It was during this time, when our group was really starting to gain traction, that Jessica found out she was pregnant again, and our convictions were put to the test.

Panic Sets in for Jessica

Jessica completed the Rachel's Vineyard retreat in the winter and, the following fall, just when the new school year was getting underway, she started texting me that she really couldn't be involved in our pro-life club any longer. She was one of our officers and so passionate about the issue, so I knew right away something was up.

As it is nowadays, many serious conversations happen over text message, and this was no different even though I tried multiple times to call her. I knew she was somewhat involved with a guy from her church, but I didn't know it had escalated to a physical relationship.

Jessica had set high standards for herself after her second abortion. She sincerely committed herself to chastity and that she ended up in the same situation again was a huge letdown for her. She had these ideals but didn't have the tools to get there – like putting up boundaries and setting limits in relationships.

The huge thing in this particular pregnancy was that the father of this baby and her weren't officially dating, and she didn't even love him. She ended their relationship and then a week later found out she was pregnant. He was not a good guy even though she had met him at church and they had enjoyed a healthy relationship at first.

Her text messages were intense and filled with panic. She just wanted out of this. Even though she was pro-life, an unplanned pregnancy just wasn't part of her plan. She was very distressed and distraught. She was working and going to school, and the same day she found out she was pregnant, she immediately called the abortion facility.

I started freaking out, and Jessica stopped texting me after unloading this bombshell. I immediately had everyone I knew praying for her and even had a professional counselor friend of mine meet with Jessica. She is half African-American and could relate better perhaps to Jessica than I could, so I was grateful for her intervention. Twenty-four hours after she told me she was pregnant, Jessica showed up at my house.

Slowly, she started opening up. I was very worried she may possibly choose abortion. She even made an appointment at the facility, but, thankfully, they didn't call her back for two weeks. I was in constant contact with her during that time, praying with her, encouraging her, and supporting her. She asked me to be the godmother of her child, and I was fairly certain she had chosen life but was still praying for her and the baby.

Birth of the Student Mothers Network

The next two months were really rough for Jessica. I was always very worried when she texted me with anxiety-ridden questions, like "How am I going to be a single mother?" Until the day she gave birth, abortion was always an option.

Jessica agreed that we could announce her pregnancy to the pro-life group on campus, and they were all so supportive, even throwing her a baby shower.

While Jessica had her friends and our pro-life group to support her, I couldn't help but think of how many other "Jessicas" were on campus who didn't have any support for their unplanned pregnancies and would not choose life. Our group had held baby showers for other pregnant students and girls on campus would just come out of the woodwork in support of these mothers, their own peers. We knew Jessica wasn't the only one in this stressful situation.

To help other pregnant moms in similar situations like Jessica's, we decided to start the *Student Mothers Network* and immediately we had another pregnant girl join, Crystyna! The three of us started having socials with a lot of food – well, because two of the three of us were pregnant.

Our group just really grew from there. We would meet every two or three weeks, but the group socials would last for like five hours. Girls started texting us and wanted to come to our socials. We posted flyers around campus advertising the *Student Mothers Network,* and, the day after we posted such a flyer, Jessica got a text from Sasha who had just found out she was pregnant and wanted to join. She is still in our group and hosts a lot of her own socials.

Today, we have about 8 to 10 parenting moms – it's been a really great support group. All of our original members have all given birth and attended each other's baby showers. The energy that came from these students was and continues to be, very powerful. Many were working while pregnant and full-time students.

These girls are amazing and continue to amaze me. Every one of them breastfed their babies and a handful even had natural births. They have become such role models for other students. They stayed in school, some have continued to work, and others help out by babysitting for each other's kids.

These mothers chose life and made the best decision for their babies and for themselves. For that freshman girl on campus who gets pregnant, she now can see this group is alive and well and that she has real support. Support is crucial when a woman faces an unintended pregnancy – to know that there are people who will affirm a mother's life-giving choice could be the decision between life and death for a preborn baby.

I don't think we will ever know the full impact the group has had on campus or how it is changing the culture of the campus and changing the stereotypes associated with being pregnant. I am glad that pregnant students now know there is a place they can go for support, and they don't have to call the abortion facility the minute they find out they are pregnant.

Spreading the Word

Even with the support Jessica had, her pregnancy was stressful. I was worried abortion was still an option up until her son was born. She asked me to be her labor coach and, after she gave birth, I just bawled. It was a huge relief. We had this little, perfect person, Stephaun, to rejoice over. He was truly a blessing.

Now whenever I meet someone that's abortion minded, I always have Jessica come with me because she has been on both sides of the fence. Without support for the girl, she can be swayed by others who want her to have an abortion. Jessica says that it was really because of her friends - myself and others - that she chose for life.

Since the start of the *Student Mothers Network,* we've been brainstorming on the idea of how to spread it to other campuses. We know the need is there, and we are anxious to help other students who are in the same position as Jessica once was.

As for the group at Sacramento State, Jessica and I are still involved with those moms. We still meet with the pregnant mothers, and the ones who have given birth have lots to share about their own babies. Jessica is now working on her master's degree, and I babysit Stephaun a few times a month while she's in class.

Because of Jessica, who reached out to our pro-life group that one fall day on campus, many babies are getting the chance at life. She has inspired not only me to work harder for the pro-life cause but so many moms who needed that extra push to choose life over abortion. And for that, I'm so grateful.

Meghan Redmond graduated in May 2011 from Sacramento State with a degree in nutrition and food degree and is an activities director at a long term care facility. She won the Students for Life of America 2011 Hans and Sophie Scholl Award and inspired SFLA's national Pregnant on Campus Initiative (www.pregnantoncampus.com). Jessica Hankerson graduated in December of 2011 from Sacramento State with a degree in child development and is currently working at a preschool as a pre-k teacher.

THE POST-ABORTIVE MOM: GWENYTH GABA

*"I was ashamed and felt I had to stay quiet about a woman's right to choose
because I had [an abortion]. That's a lie; as men and women experience
forgiveness, it gives them courage to stand up against the atrocity of abortion."*
- Georgette Forney, Silent No More

I was rubbing the gummy oils and dirt that had built up on my palms after mindlessly petting Toby for so long, and I noticed an odd peace I felt in doing so. He had wandered off to chase squirrels which gave me time to take in the moment. My mind had wandered briefly to him strutting through the garden and then back to the small brown beads in my hand.

I thought back to my old Peruvian painting professor, Javier, and what he said about this sort of thing, this sort of contemplation. He said, "There is a difference between washing your hands and being intelligent enough to see that the first level of what you are doing, physically removing the dirt, has a deeper symbol, being that you are washing away your sins."

I continued rubbing the clumps off my hand and thought, "You can't wash away your own sin."

Previously, I hadn't known why I had been acting out. "Come on, Gwenyth, get it together. What is wrong with you?!" But it felt as if something about my character, something in my spirit had died, and I would never find it again. Each day, I'd amp up what was to come, only to find at the end of it, not just my body but also my soul was weary with burdens unknown. Here I was crumbling beneath this weight, and I couldn't even place my finger on its origin.

I wanted to say it was from so many other heartaches that had happened in the process of following Jesus and losing my life, but I knew it was something else. In my relationship with Jesus there was peace, but in my relationship with myself there was extreme animosity. I hardly went a day without criticizing myself, not taking care of myself, and not pursuing healthy relationships. I saw myself withering away, and yet I couldn't stop the horrible end I saw coming.

Here is the beginning of the end of me.

My Secret

When I acted out, I hurt myself usually through random binge drinking, occasional prescription drug abuse, or I wouldn't eat. I just couldn't eat. As for these episodes, I was able to hide them, for the most part, for a matter of three years until the winter of 2012. I hadn't had an episode in so long, I figured that phase had passed. I was busy working on a film thesis project where the visuals would consist of spreading light in dark places. How ironic.

I had some floating lanterns I wanted children to release in a field with prayers attached to them. The image of illuminating the night sky with hope was romantic and visually stunning, so why not add some prayers to it? Why not dangle a few light pieces of paper to the end of each lantern?

One afternoon, I wanted to do a test run for the project so I took a few note cards and decided to write prayers, like the children would. Yet, as I was writing, my prayers became far more personal than I originally intended, and I ended up jotting down the worst things I've ever done. Who on earth knows why I decided that was a good idea?! I didn't even think about it! I just tied the prayers to the lantern and headed outside to release it. I lit the lantern, which was weighed down with my pile of sins, and let it go to complete this scene of stupidity.

As it ascended ever so slowly across the street towards my neighbor's yard, I watched in horror as it flew directly into the one large, gigantic obstacle in its path: what I've always called 'the asparagus tree.' Not a little to the left. Not a little to the right. Nope, dead on. Then, naturally, the lantern burst into flames, destroying everything except for my precious little prayers. I stood in horror.

I sprinted across the street and apologized to my neighbor, but, thankfully, by the time she came outside, the fire was out and she hadn't seen the ball of flames it was only seconds before. Now the only problem was my lantern, or rather my sins, which were oddly still intact and hanging from the charred up remains of the lantern, were stuck at the top of a tree resembling an asparagus. No branches, no nothing, until you reached about fifty feet above ground. You have got to be kidding me.

So I quickly said to my neighbor, "It was just an experiment, if it ever falls down just throw it away."

And, for what reason I cannot attest to, she asked "Are you sure you don't want it back?"

The look on my face must have given what I was thinking away, "No...it's a burned up piece of trash...I don't want it back. Please, if it falls down, throw it away." I let my stare linger a moment longer. *I'm serious, lady.*

To this, I apologized again and I left with the ever present voice whispering, "What if she does return it?" But I brushed that aside and headed home.

The next morning, I had a knock on my bedroom door.

It was my mother.

"Gwenyth...why is there this orange thing on the side of the house with a rock over it?"

I rolled over in bed and said lazily, "What are you talking about?"

She continued, "Oh, well it has this wire and it looks burned...it has your handwriting on it..."

To this, I shot out of bed. She continued, "It says something about your preborn child..."

I'm like a machine when I lie. I lied and I lied hard, "Mom, I have no idea what you are talking about! It must have been those people I was hanging out with yesterday...they have a sick sense of humor...we were debating about politics...abortion came up...you see..." *(Even I knew this sounded like crap)*.

"Well, it's in your handwriting..."

So I continued to dig the hole further, "Mom, my handwriting is miniscule- you wouldn't even be able to read it!"

And then she just asked it, "Gwenyth...did you get pregnant?"

"Mom, I do not want to talk about this!" I practically yelled. I grabbed some clothes, my purse, and I ran out the door past her.

And there it was. I had an abortion. I did something completely insane and now my own mother, the woman I was sworn to uphold some kind of decency for, knew the truth. I couldn't lie or hide or pretend my way out of this one. I felt disgustingly trapped.

The Aftermath

My favorite activity, helping out with the church's youth, was now like fire to the wound.

I couldn't look at those innocent faces around me. I couldn't speak to these young girls when I had done the worst thing a woman can do to a child. I felt like God was laughing at me. Now my mother knew, and I didn't want anyone, especially her to know.

With my secret out, this led me into a deeper depression than I had known before. I stopped helping out with the youth. I stopped going to my small group. I stopped making art. I stopped working. I stopped living.

No one told me how much an abortion would hurt. Not the church, not my family, not Planned Parenthood, not my school, not my friends, no one. They didn't tell me about this part. They didn't tell me I would be more prone to outbursts that were completely outside of my normal personality. They didn't tell me I would want to hurt myself or end my life. They never said I would become a different person. They never talked about how the love I shared with the only boy I ever loved would die with my baby. The only thing I was told was it would cost $300 dollars. They took my money and then took my baby. And the worst part is: I let them. And I would have to live with that for the rest of my life.

Facing the Truth

I knew I would have to go home soon. I couldn't sleep in my car. I did tell one person at the church, a good friend who hugged me when I told her. She didn't gasp in horror or judge me like I prayed she wouldn't. She just hugged me and prayed with me.

Eventually, it was time to drive home. I needed to talk with my mother about my outburst. To my surprise, it had started to snow. *Oh, Virginia with your random snow storms!* I got in the car and headed down the road, and then, as if a hand gently pushed my car, I slid off the road and into a ditch. I was stuck. My car was fine. I was fine. No, fine is a stupid little word - physically unharmed, I meant to say. But I was stuck. I called for a tow truck and was told I would be waiting for at least forty-five minutes before they could rescue me. And so I thought, "Well, God, you got me listening now. Go ahead. Let me have it."

See that is what I was always waiting for. For Him to really let me have it like I deserved. For His words to cut through me and destroy me as severely as I have cut through others. With fists clenched I screamed, "Come on, God! Go ahead! This is your chance! Give me your worst!"

But it was quiet. So quiet I could barely hear the soft patter of snowflakes on my windshield. The whole car was now covered except for a small circle opening the size of my hand. I felt my muscles loosen and my weight shift back into my seat. Somewhere deep down I asked, "What does this mean?" but my voice was so quiet that I didn't believe He even heard me. And then I heard it, over and over like waves, "I cover you. I cover you. Even when you are in a ditch. Even when you are in the dark. I cover you with a blanket of white snow." That's what He wanted to say.

I cannot tell you what peace I felt when I went home to tell my mother my story. She had made my favorite meal: mac and cheese and brownies. I knew why she made it. I was warming my feet by our fire, and she was trying to talk about other things when I stopped her, "Mom. I never told you because I never wanted you to be ashamed of me. I never wanted you to feel like it was your fault. It was the worst thing I've ever done, and I didn't want anyone to know. I'm so sorry." She didn't gasp in horror. She didn't look away in shame. She hugged me and made a moment of impact. I remember thinking, I never gave myself time to mourn my baby. I never thought I should be allowed to.

Surrender the Secret

I had carried the burden with me at all times, and I wasn't sure how to let it go. Even when I was having a "good" day, I never smiled quite like I used to. I wasn't always conscious of the weight of the abortion or the role it played in my life, so when I was asked to work on a reality television show called "Surrender the Secret" with the producer of October Baby, Cecil Stokes, I immediately accepted. I thought that since my mother knew and I had talked about it once, that the mourning process had hit its climax. I was wrong. It was just the beginning.

Cecil told me this was a show about how post-abortive women, going through a Bible study, would find healing from their abortions, enough so to eventually speak out about the truth of abortion. I immediately agreed to be a production assistant.

I accepted the job because I felt like I could contain my emotions. I accepted the job because I knew I needed to have more experience in filmmaking since this was my medium. I accepted the job because I was so used to the wound I carried I nearly forgot what it was like without it. I accepted the job because I am completely pro-life. That I am. I am pro-life. Yup.

How to Get Out of a Traffic Ticket

You don't have to be born of a halfwit to be a halfwit. I certainly found a way. Although I had opened up this wound, I had no idea how to fix it. So I did what I knew how to do best; I slapped a band-aid on my gushing wound and carried on.

Thinking back, I must not have thought I was doing too poorly. Surely my hangover had nothing to do with my fatal abortion decision years earlier. Oh no. I was in such a fog that I didn't even put two and two together when I randomly got trashed the night before heading to work on the reality television show. Again, my outbursts were getting worse, and yet I couldn't really understand them. So, with about one hundred dollars to my name and a headache from hell, I headed in the direction of further pain.

It was gorgeous day, completely picturesque, the wind was gentle and warm, and I stared up at the large, still clouds filling up the sky. My windows were down and my hair was whipping around in the breeze - nearly impairing my vision. Oh no! It was impairing my vision! I was blind! And what? What was that? The red and blues in my review mirror immediately formed a pit in my stomach.

Crap. All I could think was, crap. I couldn't afford a ticket. I couldn't even afford a candy bar. And right as I was headed towards excuses, I had to admit that I completely deserved it. Especially because of the night before. Especially because of all the choices I had ever made that were careless, thoughtless, and worthy of punishment.

"Ma'am, license and registration."

The officer took my information and, as he wrote me up a ticket, I stared at an old photograph of my dad when he was maybe nine or ten. I keep it in my wallet to remember him because he died when I was seven. And then I did the only thing I knew I could do in a situation like this.

"God, I know I deserve this one, but, please, please take it away. You know I can't afford this ticket. Please help me."

Even though the enemy wanted me to believe God thought very lowly of me, I knew in my heart He saw me as white as snow. I might have been a hungover halfwit, but my God remembered His covenant to His people.

"Ma'am, I'm going to need you to sign this here." The officer handed me the ticket, I signed, he handed me the receipt, and then continued to talk to me. I remember thinking, "Go away! You got what you wanted!" But he continued to tell me that up ahead the speed would change so I would need to keep my eyes peeled. I nodded but felt my tears coming. Then he asked, those fatal words, "Are you okay?" Oh crap.

He had opened the floodgates. I had burst into tears, "No...I'm....not okay! I don't have the money for this...I just want to be a filmmaker and make films for God!" Oh no. I was praying he didn't think I was one of those people who cried to get out of a ticket or used my baby blues to win a freebee.

Yet, something told me to look at him. I turned towards him as he pulled off his glasses. To my surprise, he had tears in his eyes. He said, "Let me tell you something: Within the last year my wife and my best friend were killed. Both of them would have taken a bullet for me and now I have to raise my daughter on my own. If this is going to upset you this much..." and he gently took the receipt from me, "then no one needs to know about this." And he ripped it up. "God bless you, Gwenyth Gaba." He shook my hand and walked back to his vehicle.

God is sovereign.

I'm not saying God takes away every ticket, but He took away that one.

At this point, I was wailing. Before I could fully process what had just happened, I got a call from Cecil Stokes. I could hear him smiling on the phone. He began by saying that usually he would never tell someone he hasn't met what he is about to tell me, but he felt led to tell me this. Months previously a friend of his, who has the spiritual gift of seeing of visions, told him a woman with blond hair would be a filmmaker on the set of "Surrender the Secret". Cecil believed I was meant to be there.

The Worst Choice I Ever Made

It wasn't until I was standing on the set of the reality show where women were openly discussing their abortions on national television that I realized how tender that spot was for me. I had to ask myself, what happened? Do you even remember? Yes, I remember it all.

I was nineteen. I had been dating the same boy, the only boy I ever dated, the one I wanted to marry since I was fourteen years old. I remember the night I conceived. We both felt something special had taken place that night.

I remember seeing an immediate change in my body, and, a few weeks later, I bought two pregnancy tests from a Walgreens. I remember going to my apartment, taking the tests alone, and praying to God they didn't show up as positive. But they did. Both of them did. I remember calling my boyfriend, who went to school a few hours away, and telling him to which he replied, "I'm kinda excited" and I said I was too.

I was in my freshman year of art school and he was in his sophomore year. We couldn't raise a baby. I remember going online and looking for places for me to go and have the baby and place him with an adoptive family. I remember crying on my bed and believing God could take care of us. Then I remember believing the lie that if I couldn't have him myself, it was better not to go through with it. It wouldn't hurt him. At least that is what I thought at the time.

My boyfriend tried to set me up with a counselor. I went to see a young woman associated with my college who helped counsel people in my situation. I kept saying that I knew abortion was wrong because I knew there was a child growing inside of me. She didn't say anything. I didn't feel anything when she spoke to me. She was so cold when she said, "I don't think abortion is wrong...it is what is best for the woman."

I grew up in a Christian home. I believed in God all my life, but it is remarkable how one compromise evolves into the worst decision you've ever made. I always believed abortion was wrong. Not just on a spiritual level but on a philosophical, ethical, and scientific platform. I didn't have to be a Christian to believe abortion destroys, hurts, and separates. All I had to do was live one moment in this world, breathe one breath---all I had to do was experience the gift of life to know life was worth preserving. If you've ever been thankful for your life, you know why abortion is wrong. Life is the most precious thing in the world and if humanity cannot agree on the importance of life, what can we agree upon?

But that didn't change my lack of faith. That didn't change my lack of knowledge. And that definitely didn't change the fear I felt in making any other decision than ending the life of my baby.

I was so frustrated and rushed out of the counselor's room. As I left I remember hoping, wishing someone would agree with me: abortion is wrong. Abortion is wrong. But no one did.

My boyfriend said the decision was up to me, but I knew what that meant. This way he didn't have to choose. He didn't have to feel guilty. He didn't have to take responsibility. Ultimately, I knew that he didn't want the baby right now. Of course, there would be no other time to have that specific, special, beautiful child, and yet, he didn't want him. I was completely alone. I thought that if we made this decision now we could have a baby together when we were ready. But that would never happen.

I panicked.

I felt nothing, an empty shell almost, as I went and made an appointment with Planned Parenthood. They said I was five weeks pregnant. They asked me if I wanted to see the baby during the ultrasound. I said yes.

I've thought about that image on the monitor a million times. I wish I could capture every curve and variation, because that is all I know of my baby. That and what I see in my dreams. A little blond, curly haired boy laughing. I love him so.

I came back a week later, and they gave me my prescription. It was just a series of pills to kill the baby. They made me take the first ones with them and the rest I would take on my own. I spent that weekend with my boyfriend while I was flushing out our child and felt sick the whole time. We laid on my bed and cried for our baby. He said through his tears, "This is the worst thing we've ever done." I knew then that I hadn't just killed our baby; I killed our love.

Less than a year later, the boy I loved more than anything in the world was no longer with me. I lost him, and, with him, all our friends, and yet none of that amounted to choosing not to have my baby. If I could go back, I would have chosen our child in a heartbeat.

Finding Comfort

Back in the garden with Toby, I was finishing rubbing all the dirt from my hands and wondering why I felt so much peace here. Perhaps it was because I had cried more in the past two hours than in the past three years. Or perhaps I could finally see that at the end of who I am, underneath all the secrets, is not the secret itself or the act, but the foundation is the one who made me. You can only destroy that which exists and what I did would not be the end of me.

The deepest part of me was not that I sinned but that I was created. Yes, I had sinned against God in every way one can, and I hated myself for my decisions but that was not the end of my story. God knew the lies that I and so many other women and men would listen to. He knew what sins I would commit before He created the world, yet He saw creating it as worth it. That is the glory of Christ.

That I could murder my own child, destroy everything, and yet, in Him, find forgiveness and salvation. That is love. It's a love I will never completely understand, but I am so grateful for the hope it places in my heart. The hope that this horror will end. The hope an entire generation won't be forgotten. The hope I will see my baby again, and I will tell him he is wanted and loved, and he will tell me I am forgiven. Until then, hope is what I hold onto.

Gwenyth Gaba graduated from Virginia Commonwealth University in 2012 with a BFA in Photography and Film, focus in film. She minored in Painting and Printmaking, focus in painting. She is currently a freelance filmmaker working towards her MFA in Producing.

For help after an abortion, please check out the Surrender the Secret bible study at http://www.SurrenderingTheSecret.com. Also, a schedule of Rachel's Vineyard Retreats can be found at www.RachelsVineyard.org or find a counselor at www.HopeAfterAbortion.org.

THE SURVIVOR: MELISSA PEREIRA

"The struggle of life is one of our greatest blessings. It makes us patient, sensitive, and Godlike. It teaches us that although the world is full of suffering, it is also full of the overcoming of it." - Helen Keller

**Warning: This chapter contains references to severe child and domestic abuse.*

I was in second or third grade and remember seeing blood, my mother's blood, hearing the desperate cries, and grabbing the phone to call 911. My father had found out that my mother was pregnant with a baby girl, and he was furious. He proceeded to end the pregnancy by beating her up and punching her repeatedly in the stomach. I was so little and impressionable that this gruesome memory has stayed with me my whole life. But unfortunately, it was not the only horrific memory of my childhood. My father was a monster who forced my mom to abort my two older siblings, tried to abort me and then, with his own hands, forcefully aborted what would have been the fourth child in our family, his child.

Through Hell and Back

I was born into and grew up in an abusive household. One of the earliest memories I have is from kindergarten when my dad, who was incredibly relentless and abusive, put both my mom and I into the hospital. He was a monster. As a child, I spent many nights, not knowing if I was going to see the next day. My dad would lock me in the closet for hours, and he wouldn't let me eat or go to bed. I have a permanent indent in the back of my skull because of my dad.

It wasn't until September 11, 2010 when my dad was arrested and imprisoned for a few months before a restraining order was finally put on him and my parents divorced. He was bailed out of jail and did a few stints of community service. And unfortunately, the justice system lacked any kind of assistance to my struggling, single-mother, myself and later on, my little sister. While my dad did spend some time in jail – his charges were attempted murder, battery, and assault, he was able to take a plea deal and had minimal service.

Until my dad was arrested, our lives were in turmoil. I was enrolled into Catholic school when I was young and continued through high school. It was only through the generosity and kindness of the Salesian Sisters, who ran my high school, Mary Help of Christians Academy in Northern New Jersey that I believe I made it out alive. I owe a great deal of gratitude to Sister Fran DaGrossa F.M.A, who literally journeyed with me and helped me throughout the entire ordeal.

When I entered high school, the abuse with my father heightened. When I was a junior, the abuse got really bad. I had already been taken away from my family once by the state's child protection service, and they re-entered the scene during my high school years. When I was 17 years old, I was emancipated from my parents, which was crucial to my survival. I was living on my own at 16 and learned to do my taxes by 17.

The Salesian Sisters were my saving grace during this time. They allowed me to live at the high school in dorms that were reserved for young women discerning a vocation to the religious life. They helped me get into college, and they were there every step of the way. I wanted to go to an out-of-state to school to get away from my dad and applied to Chestnut Hill College in Philadelphia. I got in and once my dad found out, he called the college and pulled my acceptance. I ended up applying and entering a nearby small liberal Catholic school, Caldwell College.

Putting the Pieces Together

When I was in sixth grade, a Life Witness team from Mary Help of Christians Academy High School came to my school and showed us a pro-life video called *The Harder Truth*, which showed pictures of abortion. The word "abortion" was always a theme in my household. My dad often told me I should have been aborted, but I did not know the meaning of the word itself. It was because of this Life Witness team that I ended up learning about abortion. After I saw this video, I knew I wanted to know more about abortion, but it wasn't until I started high school that I learned about the real aftermath of abortion and how it affects so many more people than just the mother and the baby.

In high school, I learned that abortion is one of those instances where violence breeds violence, *which of course I could easily relate to,* but I still did not know about my mother's previous two abortions.

When I joined the pro-life club at school, my dad immediately pulled me out of it. He wanted me to have nothing to do with anything "pro-life" related. I had become an officer, and I was very active. I was trying to figure out what abortion and violence had to do with each other. I was so confused.

Like a typical teenager, I rebelled against my dad and continued my pro-life involvement at school. When my dad found out I was still involved with the group, he tried to pull my registration from the school. I went to my principle and told her my dad was very abusive. The principle was able to find a sponsor for me to continue attending my high school and that is when the Salesian Sisters took me in and I literally began living at high school.

I started putting the pieces of my family together at this time. The process of emancipating from my family was lengthy, and we had to gather many police records about the incidents at my home. There was a re-occurring theme in the records - a lot of the violence happened around the times my mom was pregnant. I asked my mom about it, and it was very difficult and hard for her to discuss. She told me she had two previous pregnancies when she and my dad were really young, and, both times, my dad forced and dragged her to the local Planned Parenthood where they recommended a nearby abortion facility.

When my mom was pregnant with me and my dad found out that I was a girl, he wanted my mom to "terminate the pregnancy." My family is of Indian descent and having girls is not considered a blessing. My mom's mom, my grandmother, saved my life. She pleaded with my mom to resist her husband and to keep the child. Growing up, I stayed a lot with my grandma until she died when I was in third grade.

Because my dad didn't want my sister and me, we shouldered the brunt of his anger. When I began to learn about the aftermath of abortion and its consequences for families, I was stunned to find out that these kinds of behaviors are not only found in my own family but all across America because of abortion. It was only through the pro-life movement that I was able recognize the signs of post-abortive men and women and figure out what was going on in my home.

Going to College

At my small Catholic college, Caldwell College, I was dismayed to find out that there was no pro-life group, so I ended up starting one on my own.

Spreading the pro-life message during college was a battle. The pro-life group was handed over to someone else because I suggested we pray in front of the abortion facility and do public outreach on our campus. Apparently, those were radical activities for my Catholic campus to handle. In the interest of my desire to see the movement thrive on campus, I eventually gave up my leadership position.

I tried to get people involved in the ways that I could. My school attended the annual March for Life in Washington, D.C. and annual Students for Life of America (SFLA) Conference for the first time. It was so great to get to meet other students who were going through the same thing I was. I don't know what I would have done without them.

The scariest thing that happened to me, as a pro-lifer on campus, was the night Barack Obama was elected president in 2008. The students at my college had just voted for Barack Obama because he was cool, so in my efforts to educate my peers, I posted pictures of aborted babies on my dorm door. At the end of election night, my dorm number, my name, and other identifying information went up on Facebook and I received several threats to my well-being. I contacted SFLA and they helped me work with the campus police, who were able to find the students involved. Students for Life of America was my rock for the four years I was in college.

College was a struggle, and I graduated knowing that I did what I could to save preborn children and spread the pro-life message.

Repercussions of Abortion

The impact of one person's choice echo in different ways in people's lives. Every time I am given the opportunity, I always tell people that abortion not only ends one life, but it affects many other lives. The pro-choicers say that no one gets affected negatively by abortion, but I've endured real life situations, not hypotheticals or faulty data.'

I have managed to take my situation and use it for something positive. For me, I had the backing of the Salesian Sisters, and they became my family. My little sister has taken a different outlook on her life and was stuck at home trying to deal with our family while I was away at college. She has had a very difficult time coming to grips with our reality.

In high school and college, I suffered from night terrors and ended up going through counseling. I have read about other people like me who went through a similar situation and lost siblings to abortion having night terrors. When I was little, before I knew anything about the abortions, I had one reoccurring dream about another sibling. I don't know too much about this stuff, but I do know that sometimes when a child loses a brother or sister to abortion or even miscarriage they have a sense of someone else who was supposed to be there. I went through a period of time after I found out my siblings were aborted where I had a long stretch of guilt and questions repeated themselves in my mind like, why was I here and they weren't here?

But it was not only my little sister and I, along with my aborted siblings, who were harmed by abortion. My mom, after all her abortions, developed several health problems. She had to have an emergency hysterectomy because she was in the beginning stages of cervical cancer. Because of the abuse of my father, she suffered bodily harm as well. After going to court and finally obtaining justice for our family, she had to take time off of work and ended up losing her job. Thankfully, she recently found a new job and is slowly getting back on her feet.

Glory to God

After hearing about the abuse I suffered and growing up like I did, people usually ask me how I seem to be so normal. The secret? I've clung to my faith my whole life to get me through every moment.

While spending time as a little girl with my grandma, I was able to learn about my Catholic faith. She was the one who enrolled me in Catholic school. My dad's family is Catholic in name only and my mom's family is Hindu and Muslim. I'm so grateful to my grandmother and the Salesian Sisters for their guidance, protection, and prayers.

I'm such a strong believer in my faith and finding strength in the Eucharist and the other sacraments. It's by no coincidence that I find great resolve in knowing that I was born in October, what is officially pro-life month and that I attended a grammar school

named St. Gerard Majella, *the patron Saint of pregnancies.*
Without my faith and my convictions I could have resorted to a
number of other things to deal with the pain I was in. It's only God
who has kept me here for this long.

In college, when I got involved more in the pro-life movement and
started working with Students for Life of America, I saw a contest
to submit a pro-life video meant to influence Congress to enact
laws that protect life. It was then that I started to think about telling
my story to the public. I was so afraid people would judge me, and
I didn't want to let them into my private life yet I was given such a
huge opportunity to share my story and meet others who had lost
their own siblings to abortion. I ended up winning the video
contest, and the first month my video was posted on YouTube I got
messages from women thanking me for speaking out because they
never heard this side of the abortion story, about the kids who
survive abortion.

I have since had the opportunity to work with an organization
called Lumina who helps siblings of aborted babies deal with their
emotions and everything else they are going through. They helped
me deal with a lot of my own issues surrounding the loss of my
siblings. I am continually amazed to see how each abortion has a
rippling affect.

Shortly after my story came out, Live Action president Lila Rose
invited me to come to California, and I spent a few days with her
group. Lila is known for her undercover videos of Planned
Parenthood that show everything from the facilities helping
underage girls skirt the law to get abortions to covering up child
rape and abuse and even aiding sex trafficking. It's been amazing

meeting everyone in the pro-life movement; they have all been so supportive.

Somehow God has ignited courage in me to speak out about my story and the tragedy of abortion. I was afraid sometimes that my dad would find out that I was speaking out about this. I work in New York City now, but I live at home with my mom and my sister in Northern New Jersey and my dad lives not far away in a secluded area where registered sex offenders are only allowed to live. Whenever he moves, the police have to tell us where he is. We have a permanent restraining order against him, yet it is sometimes disheartening to know he's out there too.

I would have never thought that a little girl from Paterson, New Jersey who witnessed and lived through years of abuse would graduate from college and would work in New York City. I occasionally speak publicly and have spoken at the New Jersey Statehouse a handful of times when Planned Parenthood came through on their pink bus. I have participated in 40 Days for Life, the annual March for Life, and the celebration before the March at St. Patrick's Cathedral.

All the glory for anything I have accomplished – in fact, my mere existence after everything that I have been through – must be given back to God. For everyone that tried to protect my life, those preborn babies looking death in the face deserve someone to stand up for them.

Melissa Pereira graduated from Caldwell College in May 2012.

THE ADOPTED DAUGHTER AND BIRTHMOTHER: ANDREA ARTZ

"Mother love is the fuel that enables a normal human being to do the impossible." - Marion C. Garretty

I am adopted.

Growing up, I had complete knowledge about my adoption. As I asked questions, my mother answered them in detail. In our kitchen, we have a framed quote that reads, "Adoption is proof that prayers are answered." This is exactly how my mother explains my adoption to everyone. Her prayers to God were answered when she learned that she had an opportunity to adopt, even as a single parent, a baby from Peru – me.

I was five weeks old the first time we met. My mom and I call it my "Gotcha Day." My mom spent three days with my birthmother while she was in Peru to adopt me. During this time my mom thanked her, loved her, and appreciated her for the selfless decision she made for me. My birthmother knew that she couldn't give me the best life possible, so she decided to make an adoption plan. She wanted one thing for me more than anything else: an education.

Growing up in Saint Louis, I have been *so* privileged. I went to Catholic grade school and high school and now college. I have been to Washington D.C. for the pro-life March for Life four times, *twice* after having knee surgery. I have been on numerous vacations over the years. I have a very stable home environment. I have a very supportive, close-knit family who I can count on to be there for me, no matter what happens. They are literally a phone call and a few houses away because we all live in the same neighborhood. And I have a *better-than-life* relationship with my mom. It is an understatement to say I am blessed.

My adoption has always been viewed in a positive way. My mom not only wanted me to experience American life, she also wanted me to get to know my Peruvian heritage. One way she ensured this when I was young was to enroll me in Peruvian dance classes where I met many other Peruvian children who were also adopted. Meeting, getting to know, and spending time with these families helped me to embrace and appreciate my adoption. Adoption is also celebrated in my family. Every November, during National Adoption Month, my mom and I go to an Adoption Mass at the St. Louis Cathedral Basilica, where families touched by adoption gather and receive a blessing. It was and still is a beautiful sight to see the love adoption provides to families.

I consider myself lucky to have two mothers: a mother who gave birth to me and a mother who raised me. I know my amazing life has been a gift, and being pro-life is something that has simply been ingrained in me since I was young and I have always been proud of it.

Getting Pregnant

I had my heart set on going to Benedictine College in Kansas after I graduated high school. The school had a vibrant faith community and that was an aspect of my life I wanted to strengthen. It was also five hours away from home, so I knew homesickness couldn't be avoided. Nevertheless I was looking forward to a new adventure.

The summer before my freshmen fall semester, I met a guy. It was stupid and nothing serious. We weren't even "boyfriend-girlfriend," but I ended up losing my virginity to him. In my Catholic high school, we talked a lot about chastity, and overall, it was basically a "sex-waits-for-marriage" approach. This suited me just fine because I thought I was going to wait for marriage, or, at least, someone I loved. But, I didn't. It was a one-time thing with the guy, who I did not love and was not in a relationship with. Thinking back, the person who made this irresponsible choice was not the *me* that I know.

Putting two-and-two together, I knew there was a possibility of pregnancy because I was not on birth control and he did not use a condom. Having no idea what to do and also wanting to confide in someone, I told two of my best friends what had happened. They both suggested and agreed to take me to Planned Parenthood to purchase the morning after pill. Being naïve and trusting that my friends knew how to handle this situation, I did just that. The whole time I understood that the morning after pill could prevent a pregnancy from occurring but also could cause an early abortion if I had already conceived, but my friends told me that wasn't likely.

My friends picked me up before work the next day, and we drove to the closest Planned Parenthood. We walked in, and immediately I felt so out of place. The receptionist only took my first name and we had to wait ten minutes for a $40 pill. I didn't have the money, so I stole it from my mom without her knowledge *(horrible, I know)*. Planned Parenthood's only instructions were that I had to take the pill with a meal. My friends drove me back home, acting as if this trip to Planned Parenthood was no big deal.

My boss took me out to lunch that day, and I had a huge meal. I thought this was a good opportunity to take the pill, but my conscious was making me question if *I* wanted to take it or my friends wanted me to. What if I took this pill and it ended a pregnancy that was already there? I whole heartedly believe that life begins at the moment of fertilization, so I knew that taking the tiny pill clearly went against what I believed to be true. I could take this pill up to six days past sexual intercourse; therefore, I had that time to decide what to do next.

What I really was waiting for was someone to tell me not to take it.

Taking the Pill or Not?

That evening after work, I called one of my friends and asked her what to do. She thought I should take it. Not satisfied and still confused, I called my friend Terrie. I told her the whole story. Then she told me exactly what I wanted to hear, "Andrea, you know if you take it, it is against your beliefs. *Don't take it.*" That was it. That was all I needed. I did not take the morning after pill. I was so incredibly grateful for Terrie's advice and encouragement.

The Saturday night before Father's Day, I stayed up thinking about what might actually happen if I was pregnant. It occurred to me, after watching some episodes of *"Teen Mom,"* that I would want to make mature parenting decisions. And the only way I saw this being fulfilled was to make an adoption plan. That night, June 21, 2009, I wrote for the first time, in a long time, in my prayer journal:

> *Dear God, I'm not close with you anymore. I have always believed that things happen for a reason. I have always believed you have a plan for each one of us. Please help me*

to follow the plan that you have for me. That is all I ask.
Thank you for my mothers who gave me life. Love, Andrea

I ended up going to Mass the next morning, much to the happiness of my mother who had gone the night before without me. She thought I was being such a good daughter, but in reality, I needed to spend time with God at mass.

I had accepted that if I was pregnant, I was going to make an adoption plan. It was a huge relief, and I felt like I was making the right choice. But now I had to wait it out to see if I was pregnant and then I had to figure out how to tell my mom if I was.

Telling my Mom

Before going away to college I had to have a physical exam. The doctor and nurses asked me all the typical questions, including if I was sexually active. If sexually active meant a one-time thing, then I guess I was. They asked if I wanted a pregnancy test, and I said yes. The doctor, who I had only met that day, walked in and exclaimed, "Andrea Andrea Andrea, you're pregnant." I started sobbing.

I immediately called my mom, who could tell something was wrong. Her office was only five minutes away. I told her I needed to tell her something and that I would come right over. When I got to her office, she sent someone down to the lobby to get me, and we had to ride in the elevator together. I was a mess, and it was awkward, to say the least.

I told my mom straight out I was pregnant. She knew I didn't have a boyfriend or was someone that ever brought boys home, so she was shocked. She raised me with good morals and values, so understandably she had a lot of questions. She told me we would talk further when she got home.

I wasn't the only one with big news at the time. My mom was already under a lot of stress because she had just found out that her job was in jeopardy. As a single mother who had just found out her daughter was pregnant, it was a whirlwind of emotion for her.

She couldn't handle the news alone, so she called her sister. Aunt Sherry, who lived six houses down the street, drove over immediately. She knew something was wrong. When my mom told her I was pregnant, my aunt said it was ok. She didn't freak out, which made me feel a little better.

The three of us decided I would stay home to attend college, so, instead of going to Benedictine, I would attend Fontbonne University in the fall. I was devastated, but I knew there was no way I was going to be able to do this by myself and at a school five hours away. Moreover, I didn't want to tell anyone I was pregnant. Since I felt so ashamed, I did what I could to hide the pregnancy.

My mom was really supportive after she got over the shock. I told her I wanted to make an adoption plan, and she was surprised to learn I had made up my mind so quickly. But I already had time to think about what I was going to do when I was deciding whether or not to take the pill and then waiting to see if I was pregnant or not. I now knew I had a life inside me, which helped put my adoption plans into motion.

Hiding the Pregnancy

My aunt is the one who told my extended family I was pregnant. As expected, my family was in shock, but they kept all their questions quiet, at least around me. They never acknowledged my pregnancy or said anything about it to me. I knew my pregnancy was an awkward situation, but their silence made me feel like I wasn't even part of the family anymore. My closest cousins cancelled plans, and at family dinners, instead of talking to me, I was left out of the conversation. In a way, I understood that they needed time to process the news of my pregnancy, but I was still the same person, just a pregnant person.

A cousin of my mine found out she was pregnant four months before I did. While she could be publicly happy about her pregnancy, I was hiding mine. That was really hard for me, probably the most difficult part of the entire process. She was so happy at family gatherings. She and her growing belly were the center of attention, while I was hiding my little life growing inside, ashamed of what I'd done.

My mom was there for me the entire time. She made sure I was covered under her insurance. She gave me a booklet that explained how my baby was developing during the pregnancy. It told me what and what not to eat in order to keep healthy. She also came with me to most of my doctor appointments. Since I couldn't talk to any of my family members, I would just let it all out on my mom, and it was good being able to talk to her. I was incredibly grateful for my mom because she supported me throughout this tumultuous time.

I didn't tell any of my friends from high school why I changed schools or that I was pregnant. I just told them I was staying home for school.

School and Adoption Planning

I started classes at Fontbonne University in the fall with my due date approaching quickly in March. I knew a few people there from my high school, but no one knew I was pregnant. I didn't go to too many of the orientation events because I worried someone would find out I was expecting – I was unnecessarily paranoid. I only made a few good friends during my freshman year. I didn't want to tell anyone I was pregnant.

I heard about a Christian retreat held by my university called *Metanoia* that my friend Lauren told me about. I decided I needed to go on it to get away from school and family. I needed a weekend to get closer to God. On the *Metanoia* retreat, there was time set aside to talk to someone one-on-one. I pulled Lauren aside and unloaded the secret of my pregnancy and my adoption choice.

She told me I was so strong for making a selfless choice in the midst of a difficult situation. Talking to Lauren gave me a sense of relief and increased my self-esteem. At 21 weeks along, I found out I was having a baby girl. My mom and I named her Rosie. Since Lauren knew of my pregnancy, I was able to share this news with her. It was nice to be able to give her baby updates. For the first time, I felt supported by a friend, which was very comforting.

I ended up telling another friend, Terrie – the one who convinced me not to take the morning after pill - but not until after I had my daughter.

In my second trimester, I contacted the same adoption agency my mom went through to adopt me. I sent them an email saying I was pregnant with a bi-racial baby girl and wanted to place my baby for adoption. They contacted me the next day, and I soon met my social worker, Linda. The first few meetings with Linda were meant as a means to establish a good relationship with each other. I told her immediately about my background as an adoptee, and that I wanted to make the same decision my birthmother had made for me.

I knew that if I chose to parent Rosie, I would struggle to provide for her every need and want. I would need to make a lot of sacrifices; and, yet, I would still only be able to provide the bare minimum. I could rely on my mom, but she already raised a child on her own. Of course, I could provide unconditional love, but love isn't the only thing you need to parent a child and still give them everything they need. My dream is to be a mother, but I knew it wasn't my time yet.

Over the next few months, I met with Linda regularly. In December, I asked to look at adoptive parent profile packets. I wanted to be prepared for this decision. If at all possible, I wanted to meet Rosie's adoptive family before her birth. Linda said it was too soon, so we held off at looking at the packets.

Christmas came and went. I went back to school in the spring semester, and I had a couple night classes. My cousin, who I had been close with before my pregnancy, had night classes too.

Sometimes after class we had a late night dinner at Applebees – like old times. I really enjoyed the opportunity to be close with her again and the honest conversations we had about my pregnancy.

On January 20th, when I was almost 32 weeks along, my cousin and I went to Applebee's and enjoyed a late dinner. Afterwards we drove home separately. As I was driving home, my water broke. It startled me, and I had no idea what was happening. After thinking that I had peed my pants, I finally realized that my water broke! My mom and I went to the hospital the next morning, and the doctors confirmed my water did indeed break.

I was checked into a private hospital room right away. To ensure Rosie's health, I was given steroids to help her lungs and other organs to develop, in the case that I did go into preterm labor. Through it all, I remained surprisingly calm. I had no idea that early the next morning I would deliver a preterm baby girl.

That night, I emailed my teachers and explained to them what I was hoping to tell them eight weeks later. I was worried that my teachers would judge me, but I knew I had to explain my situation since I would be absent from classes. Their kind reactions pleasantly surprised me. They gave me ample time to catch up on my work and kept me in their prayers. I couldn't have asked for better support.

I went into labor later that night. As the contractions intensified, I called my mom, who had gone home to get some sleep and take a shower. She said she'd be right there, but I told her not to worry – not realizing how close I was to delivering. Being the loving mother that she is, she, thankfully, came right away. And fortunately the doctor walked in the room immediately after my mom did. As it turned out, they both got there in the nick of time; minutes later I gave birth to my miracle baby girl, Rosie.

Rosie

Rosie was born on January 22 – the anniversary of *Roe v. Wade* and *Doe v. Bolton*, the two Supreme Court decisions that legalized abortion throughout all nine months of pregnancy, for whatever reason.

After letting me hold Rosie very briefly, the doctors took her to the Neonatal Intensive Care Unit. My mom and I were left in the delivery room where we talked about how beautiful Rosie was. As we talked, I dozed in and out periodically, out of sheer exhaustion. My first thought when I woke up was of Rosie and how much I wanted to see her. My mom and I went to the NICU right away, where I got to see and hold her.

Rosie was lovely. She had a full head of black hair and beautiful dark eyes. She had soft caramel colored skin. She weighed three pounds and fourteen ounces. As tiny as she was, she was the picture of perfection. I held her close to me, and it felt so good to be holding this gift from God. The nurse suggested that I put her inside my shirt and hold her close to my heart. That is what they call kangaroo care, which is skin-to-skin contact with baby and mom. It was surreal. Here I was, holding this tiny baby in my arms. That was the moment I realized that *I was a mother.*

I knew I was only going to be in the hospital for a day after I gave birth, so I made sure to visit the NICU as much as I could during that time. I was only able to hold Rosie for thirty minutes each time because she was so fragile and needed to be in an incubator.

My whole family came to visit Rosie. They knew I was making an adoption plan, but their visits demonstrated their love for me. They knew how much I needed their support.

When I got home from the hospital, I felt so empty. I was used to having Rosie kicking me at all hours of the day. Now she wasn't there anymore. I knew she was safe at the hospital being monitored by nurses, but I needed a physical closeness to reassure me that she was okay.

I got into a routine where my aunt would pick me up after she got off work at noon and take me to the hospital to see Rosie. When my mom got off work, she'd come to pick me up, but not until she visited for an hour or two. We did this every day for two weeks. Our weekends were spent at the hospital with Rosie. During this time, we fed Rosie, burped her, changed her diapers, sang to her, and rocked her to sleep.

My mom enjoyed being a grandma. I loved being a mom.

I kept in touch with my teachers and some of them said I could catch up later. My doctor had given me a note to take off six weeks from school. Since I didn't want to fall behind, I only took two. When I went back to school, I would go to the NICU to spend time with Rosie in between classes. It became a ritual to spend as much time with her as possible.

I didn't know this at the time, but it's peculiar for a birthmother to spend all that time with her baby. Some of the nurses were surprised and wondered if I would change my mind about the adoption. While I knew in my heart that the adoption plan was the best choice for Rosie and me, there were many tears shed as the bond between Rosie and I grew stronger each day. My mom and I both fell deeply in love with this beautiful angel.

While my family visited Rosie right after she was born, they didn't understand why I wanted to see Rosie every day. They, too, worried I might change my mind. Once they saw that I really loved her and was set in my decision though, they came to accept what I was doing.

Throughout my visits with Rosie, I was in contact with my social worker, Linda. We agreed that it was finally time to look at prospective adoptive parent profile packets. She gave my mom and me eight adoption profiles to look over. I flipped the stack and read the first one. This one immediately spoke to me, as she was a single woman who seemed to be very much like my mom. I read the others but kept going back to the first profile. I knew then she would be Rosie's adoptive mom. Choosing the adoptive family was a major step in making an adoption plan for Rosie, numbering my days I would have left with my daughter.

After I made the decision, we headed back to the hospital where I met Tresa, a nurse. She came up to me as I arrived in the NICU and said, "You're doing the right thing." Without even knowing it, Tresa affirmed my decision that I was doing what was best for Rosie. That day had been so tough for me. As I was going through the profiles of prospective adoption parents, my emotions had seesawed. While I knew I wanted to make the adoption plan, I was going back and forth because I realized I wouldn't see Rosie after I placed her with an adoptive family.

Rosie and I bonded with Tresa instantly. She was so great to the both of us, making sure Rosie had nice blankets, was dressed in cute preemie clothes, and had bows in her hair. Tresa's words and actions showed that she really cared about us. My mom and I both believe that Tresa was truly an angel sent to us by God.

Rosie's Adoptive Mom

Too soon the time came for us to meet Rosie's adoptive mom and her family. A meeting was scheduled at the adoption agency. My mom and I were anxious to meet them but, at the same time, nervous. We hoped that the woman we saw in the profile would be the right one to raise our precious Rosie.

Our anxiety was soon put to rest when we met Kelly. She immediately bonded with us and we knew she would make a great mother. She had similar values to ours; being a Catholic convert, she said Rosie would be raised Catholic. She was a pediatric nurse practitioner and was used to working with children who faced challenges in their lives. After meeting Kelly, it was now more than a profile on a piece of paper. It was mother choosing mother. Kelly and I spent a great deal of time together sharing pictures of Rosie. We also shared information about our own lives and bonded as well. By the end of the day, we felt like we had known each other and, more importantly, cared about each other. After all, we were about to be sharing something so important - a precious little life.

Like my own birth mother who spent five weeks with me before I was placed for adoption, I spent a couple more weeks with Rosie. She was finally released from the NICU but instead of me taking her home, Linda suggested that Rosie live with foster parents until the adoption was finalized.

These particular foster parents, Mary Jo and Mike, had been foster parents for 20 years and had taken care of over 60 babies during that time. They, too, were a gift to Rosie and me. They were a warm, understanding couple who opened their home, not only to Rosie, but to me and my mom as well. They allowed us visit Rosie at their house, which was highly unusual given the circumstances. We went over every other evening and again spent time holding Rosie and loving her. Mary Jo and Mike made us feel very welcome in their home and in their hearts. And as the adoption drew closer, Kelly and her mom were also allowed to visit Rosie at Mike and Mary Jo's.

By now it had been five weeks since Rosie had been born. I felt as close to her as any mother could feel to her child. My love for her had grown with each day, and she had taken up permanent residence in my heart. But the time had come to finalize the adoption.

We had an entrustment ceremony which is where the birth parents, the adoptive parents and the foster parents come together for a prayer service. The purpose of the ceremony was to show that we were all coming together for the sake of the baby and wanted what was best for her. I held Rosie the entire time, and she slept like a little angel.

At the end, I handed over Rosie to Kelly, and that is when I lost it. I couldn't hold back the tears. It was the last time I got to hold my little girl. My consolation was that I knew how much my mom had wanted to raise a baby and got that chance because of my birth mother, and now I was giving Kelly that same chance because of my choice.

I chose a semi-open adoption plan which meant that for the first six months, I got pictures and a letter every month. And after those six months, I will receive pictures and a letter three times per year. I asked Kelly to please keep "Rose" as a part of Rosie's name, and she did. And that made me very happy. A rose is the most beautiful flower that God has given us. And our little Rose was the most beautiful flower God could have given me.

After the Adoption

The first month was very difficult. I was used to holding Rosie and loving her, and I missed her with all my heart. I wanted to enjoy feelings of happiness, having made the best decision for Rosie and me, but I had a period of grieving to get through first. I busied myself with my college classes and worked through one day at a time. Time itself is a healer. While my love for Rosie will never diminish, my happiness for her new life keeps growing.

The next semester, I became a member of several campus organizations. One was campus ministry, which allowed me to attend the Metanoia retreat. This was the same retreat I had gone on while I was pregnant. And this time I was invited to give a talk, called "Taking the Risk." It was the first time I told my story. I was terrified I would be judged, but I could not have been more wrong. Instead I received support, words of encouragement, and prayers from everyone on the retreat.

When I was a sophomore at Fontbonne, I met Sheri from Students for Life of America. She ended up giving me all the information and tools I needed to start a pro-life club on campus. With the help of my friends, we were able to start an official campus pro-life group, and we plan on going to the March for Life in 2013, which will be commemorated on Rosie's birthday, January 22nd.

I've since given more talks at Metanoia retreats as well as at adoption panels. While it's easy to share my story on a retreat, it's not always as easy to share my story with friends. My mom and I have a rule of thumb – tell those who love me and who will not use the beautiful story of Rosie as a form of gossip. Rosie and I deserved better than that.

Soon after the adoption I felt like I needed to talk to another birth mother who had gone through what I went through. Linda gave me the number of a girl named Annie, but I never called her.

However, six months after Linda gave me her number, I went to the St. Louis Cathedral's annual Adoption Mass, and I asked Linda to come with me. During the Mass, Linda leaned over to me and told me that Annie was sitting right behind us. After Mass, I met Annie, and she offered to go out to lunch. It only took me two months to get up the courage to call her, and it turns out we have so much in common – our due dates were the same except in different years, we gave birth in the same hospital, and we go to the same school. Perhaps the coolest part is that Annie has a son named Will, and our babies are friends!

Annie and I both wanted to go to the *On Your Feet* Foundation Retreat for birth mothers but ended up not making the cut because so many moms signed up. So we decided to hold our own retreat instead that we planned with our social workers. It was wonderful, and we had eight birth mothers who signed up. Thoughout this process, I've learned that it's been very important to have support from other birth mothers who have been through the same thing as me. On Birth Mother's Day, which is the weekend before Mother's Day, we all had our nails done to celebrate.

Life Goes On

Spending four weeks with Rosie was a blessing for me. I would not trade that time for anything in the world. Having that time together allowed me to come to terms with making the adoption plan. It gave me time to truly realize what was best for her. The semi-open adoption has proved to be a good decision for me. I get so excited when I receive those pictures and letters from Kelly.

I'm so grateful I was able to give life to Rosie. In so doing, I was able to share this beautiful gift with another person, just as my birth mom shared the gift of my life with my mom. Rosie is very blessed. She has two mothers who love her and want only the best for her.

Rosie will be three years old come January 2013. She is absolutely adorable. She would melt any heart. She has a smile that lights up a room and lights up my life every time I see her picture.

My plans for the future are to complete my education and become a teacher. Some days are harder than others. I miss Rosie, but I know she is where she is meant to be. More than anything I look forward to the day when she chooses to meet me, her birthmother. I hope she will know just how much I love her. On that day, I will tell her.

Andrea is a senior at Fontbonne University in Missouri and is getting her degree in elementary education. She will be starting her student-teaching in the spring of 2013.

YOUR CALL TO BE COURAGEOUS: KRISTAN HAWKINS

*"If to be feelingly alive to the sufferings of my fellow-creatures is to be a fanatic,
I am one of the most incurable fanatics ever permitted to be at large."*
- William Wilberforce

"Bye Mommy, I loves you."

These are words I dread to hear in the morning. I usually like to leave the house before my sons, Gunner and Bear, are awake, so I don't have to hear these words. It breaks my heart leaving the house and heading to work. Every time, I am on my laptop and my son Gunner says "No! Don't work," a little pain constricts.

I love my children and they are the best thing I have ever done in my life. They truly are God's greatest miracle.

Yet, I have to leave them for work. Not just any work but pro-life work. My "job" isn't a 9 to 5 job - it's a 24-7 crusade to grow Students for Life of America and empower this generation to abolish abortion in our lifetime.

Despite the incredible opportunity I have been given with SFLA, I never really believed that my life was anything extraordinary to write about. I was raised in a middle-class, white, Christian family. Nothing overly traumatic happened to me during my childhood. I met my husband my first day in high school. I've always been a Christian.

I never really thought about abortion that much until I was asked to volunteer at a pregnancy resource center one summer during high school. I thought I was just going to this "women's center" to help answer phones and organize the supply room. I had no idea that in just a few weeks I would be empowered to save a life as I would be talking to women who believed abortion was their only option.

But I've been wrong. You see, my life is extraordinary. Because like the young people featured in this book and like you, I was chosen, just like you, by the Creator of the Universe, to do extraordinary, life-saving works through Him.

And right now, as we live in the 40th year of legal abortion in United States, the time has come for our movement to declare that we will abolish abortion in our lifetime. And working through Him, it's possible.

Time is of the essence as we have lost too many already. Over 54 million preborn boys and girls, who just like you are intrinsically valuable because they were made in His image, have been thrown in the trash because their mothers were deceived and told that they couldn't keep their babies and continue their educations, provide for their families, or keep their relationships together.

I know that 54 million is an impossible number to get your head around. It is more deaths than all casualties of wars our nation has suffered. More than any disease, more than during the Middle Passage when Africans were abducted and forced into slavery, and more than the Holocaust. But think of it in another way.

If you were born after January 22, 1973, you are a survivor of legal abortion. We've survived legal abortion, but a third of our generation did not. People God had intended as our best friends, siblings, boyfriends, girlfriends, wives, and husbands did not make it.

There is reason for joy though, and I hope you can feel it after reading through this book, because the tide is turning in America. More Americans now than ever recognize that abortion is wrong and kills an innocent human being. And I believe God, the Creator of the universe and maker of all, is calling our movement today, more than ever before, to be his hands and feet to abolish abortion in our lifetime.

But to fulfill this mission of abolishing abortion, we must do three things: **pray**, **envision**, and then **engage**, guided by our courageous love and spirit.

Now, Students for Life is a secular organization, but, if you believe in a higher power like I do, I encourage you to pray first.

Pray that the hearts of our nation's leaders and those whom we elect would be moved to protect all Life. Abolishing abortion will not happen solely through politics, but abolishing all abortion will not happen unless laws are changed.

Next, pray for those who work against us. Those Planned Parenthood employees and those involved daily in the aborting of children, the church member who you know is involved in electing only pro-abortion, pro-infanticide candidates, your neighbor who donates to pro-abortion organizations and has a Planned Parenthood bumper sticker on her car, and those who work in our government who believe that freedom of religion and conscience is a notion from the past.

Then, pray for the preborn and their mothers and fathers. Pray for those parents who want to keep their child but fear the uncertain economic conditions surrounding their family. Pray for that single mother who fears her boyfriend's reaction and believes that she has no other choice than to kill her precious child. Pray for that high school or college student who is considering breaking her promise to save sex until marriage and pray for that girl when she takes the test and sees those tiny blue lines.

And finally, pray and ask our Savior where He wants you, an ordinary person with already too many things you are responsible for, to engage in this epic battle. Pray that he gives you the perseverance and courage necessary to fulfill His plan for your life.

Now, we know that in order to end abortion we must make great strides in future elections and we have to continue to move forward de-funding the abortion industry and making abortion unprofitable. But we also have to do more than that - we have work to make abortion unthinkable by every mother and father. And all of this starts with one simple concept, my second action item: envision.

Envision, not imagine, what our nation will look like without legal abortion.

Imagine a high school football coach telling his team that they couldn't win before running onto the field. What would the result be? Do you think the team would have any chance of winning? No, of course not. Yet, that is precisely what happens when I talk to many people about engaging in the pro-life movement, some of them even leaders. And you know these people yourself - it might be you, your pastor, your friend, your husband, or neighbor. They believe abortion, while evil, will always happen. They have lost the urgency, resolve, and passion each of us needs to fight this war against of the Culture of Death, day in and day out.

For those who have lost this urgency and passion, I have one simple question: I expect big and great things from my awesome God. Do you?

When David volunteered to face off with Goliath, what happened? His faith and a few small stones provided him with all that he needed.

Envision means that we must make our plans for **post-Roe America now**– to support and establish the structures, all across our nation that we will need to make sure no woman and family gets left behind.

In order to end abortion in our nation, we must first be able ourselves to envision a nation, where every woman facing a unplanned, crisis pregnancy knows that there is a place near her that she can turn to for help.

Transforming our nation and ending abortion starts with envisioning its end. See what it looks like in your mind's eye, believe it yourself, and then make the plan and set out to work, guided by your courageous love.

This is the third step: engage. Trust me, there are many ways you can get to work and engage in the pro-life movement. Get started right in your community.

Start a pro-life group at your local high school or college in order to educate and help those most targeted by the abortion industry, get involved electing only pro-life public officials, work to change the hearts of our neighbors and family members, lobby your state legislators to pass state laws which will protect the preborn and their mothers, get your pastor or priest on board to activate your church or parish, financially support national and local pro-life organizations, or volunteer at a pregnancy help center to provide the emotional support and tangible resources women need to choose life.

I can't tell you how many times women have said to me that they wouldn't have had their abortion if only one person had encouraged them not too. Only a few kind words could have saved her baby. And you can do that, you can be that person or you can help empower a young person or someone else to do it on your behalf.

The time is now to engage and engage courageously, because surrender is not an option.

Be courageous.

- o Have the courage you need to finally talk with your neighbor, father in law, or friend and ask them why they are voting for pro-abortion political candidates.

- o Have the courage to ask your priest or pastor to speak about the evil of abortion and healing power of the Savior.

- o Have the courage to offer to pray with your sister who you know had an abortion a few years ago.

- o Have the courage to drive to your local abortion facility and peacefully pray in front of the facility and offer women entering an alternative to the killing.

- ○ Have courage when your daughter or granddaughter comes to you and tells you she has made a mistake and is pregnant; don't urge her to have an abortion simply because you may fear how it will look to others.

- ○ Have the courage to finally start that prayer group in church for those needing healing after abortion or finally start volunteering at the women's help center.

- ○ Have the courage to start that pro-life group in your high school or college.

Be courageous like Meghan, Melissa, Steve, Julia, Billy, Andrea, Caroline, Gwenyth, Gina, Chaunie, Amanda, and Rebekah.

Today is the day that you are being called to courageously abolish abortion and rise up. Rise up off the couch, out of your dorm room, and off of your pew. Because today, tomorrow, and the next day, there are babies who are scheduled to die and mothers whose heartbreak is certain.

Act now to pray, envision, and engage. Only He knows the precise date of when abortion will be made illegal in our land. But He has a plan, and we have been called to be part of it and to do our part in abolishing abortion.

I challenge you today: dedicate your short time here on earth, your life, to something bigger than yourself. Act courageously, despite where your fears or comfort ability may lie, and be His hands and feet- no matter what the costs.

Act now and courageously abolish abortion for you were chosen.

WHAT WE DO AT
STUDENTS FOR LIFE OF AMERICA
www.studentsforlife.org

Field Program

The SFLA Field Program is what truly sets SFLA apart from other student and pro-life organizations across America. We are engaging students on campuses; building relationships with the generation that will abolish abortion; and training leaders to change hearts, change minds, and save lives. We know that pro-life student groups are making a difference because we track and measure our progress and the accomplishments of each groups. Since 2006, SFLA has helped start more than 523 groups and is currently working with over 706 active groups. The SFLA Field Program consists of full-time Regional Coordinators who work in specific regions across the nation to start *and* improve pro-life groups on college campuses. We are there for pro-life students when and where they need the most.

Training and Resources

Students for Life of America is the "one-stop shop" for any student pro-lifer. SFLA provides students of all ages with all the training, materials, support, and resources they need to do anything and everything pro-life. We have activism guidebooks, ready-to-go events with step-by-step guides, sample flyers, and more. We also provide free Skype, in person, or over the phone trainings to pro-life students on topics such as Activism, Leadership Identification and Development, Membership Recruitment and Retention, and Creating a Vision and Strategy. Our goal is to give students the training, resources, and information they need to lead successful pro-life organizations on campus.

SFLA National and Regional Conference

On January 22, 2012, SFLA sold out its 25th Annual National
Conference with 1,900 attendees, representing over 167 schools,
97 Students for Life groups and 2 international groups – making
the event the largest pro-life conference in the nation. With over
40 different pro-life organizations participating and a myriad of
pro-life professionals presenting on the current Life issues facing
our nation, SFLA student leaders were both educated and inspired
to return to their campuses and make a difference.

Every January, SFLA hosts it's National Conference in
Washington, D.C. around the time of the annual March for Life.
Each semester, SFLA hosts Regional Training Days for students
that focus on personal leadership skills and group development.

Med Students for Life

Med Students for Life (MedSFL), launched during the 2011-2012
school year, is the only national network of future medical
professionals committed to improving quality health care by
defending conscience rights and every human life. By the end of
the 2011-2012 school year, Med Students for Life had groups at 35
of the 162 medical schools in the United States. With the lives of
thousands of preborn children at stake, MedSFL hopes to continue
to grow and expand in the coming years and directly counter the
abortion industry's grip on our nation's med school campuses.

Pregnant on Campus

The *Pregnant on Campus Initiative*, launched during the
2011-2012 school year, aims to provide a vision and plan to the
campus pro-life groups which seek to establish service projects to

help women and families on campus and in the community. Our goal is to reduce abortion rates on college campuses by creating service projects that provide essential resources and policies for fellow students facing unplanned, crisis pregnancies.

New Media

Students for Life works hard to meet students where they are, including online. SFLA can be found on Facebook, Twitter, YouTube, and Pinterest. In addition to social networking sites, SFLA sends out weekly e-mail messages to students about upcoming national pro-life events as well as the many educational opportunities available to them.

Missionaries for Life

SFLA's highly-competitive summer internship program, known as *Missionaries for Life*, selects the best and brightest pro-life college leaders from around the country and brings them to the Washington, D.C. area for a 9-week program involving 3 rotations. The goal is to give aspiring pro-life leaders the opportunity to experience what it's like to work in the pro-life movement full-time and to find their niche in this human rights cause.

Wilberforce Leadership Fellowship

This *Wilberforce Leadership Fellowship* is designed to teach leadership skills to the top student pro-life activists considering a full-time career in the pro-life movement through leadership readings and discussion, bi-weekly webcasts with national pro-life leaders and businessmen, and a mentoring relationship with a national pro-life leader.

Special Projects

Students for Life of America is a grassroots organization in tune with what is happening in our nation. Because SFLA has a close connection with student groups and our team is passionate about our unique mission, we can respond at a moment's notice as events develop across the country. In 2012 alone, SFLA's activism in Washington, D.C. was featured on all the major TV news networks.

CONNECT WITH SFLA

www.studentsforlife.org
www.facebook.com/studentsforlife
www.twitter.com/students4lifehq
www.youtube.com/studentsforlife

info@studentsforlife.org